Foreword

"THE unknown God." The men of Athens in the days of St. Paul were a little afraid that despite their knowledge of not a few "gods" there might yet be one "god" whom they were neglecting. They therefore erected an altar to him and offered him their "devotions". St. Paul saw them so engaged as he "passed by". He seized upon that inscription, and used it as a text from which to preach Christ. "Whom therefore ye ignorantly worship," he cried, "Him declare I unto you", Acts 17. 22, 23. Would the apostle not be constrained to say similar things to some of us?

How much do you know about God? THE UNKNOWN GOD. It is not that we have never *heard* of Him, or known about Him. But do we truly KNOW Him? Do we take as much trouble and interest in *knowing God*, and His marvellous working in human hearts and lives, as we do about our wireless set, or about the technique of our favourite sport? Do we even know that our eternal destiny depends upon *knowing God*?

Now the Lord Jesus Christ is a perfect revelation of what God is like. Did He not say, "He that hath seen Me hath seen the Father"? John 14. 9. Yes, our Lord was perfect God and perfect man. But how *much* do you and I know *about* Jesus Christ? Have we ever taken the trouble—the *pleasure*—of reading the Bible in order to find out all we can about the Saviour? Are we even aware that the knowledge of Christ Jesus our Lord is set down in the Scriptures as the purpose of all that we call "life"?

Our blessed Lord, communing with the Father, said to Him in the hearing of His apostles: "This is life eternal that they might know Thee, the only true God, and Jesus Christ, Whom Thou hast sent", John 17. 3.

The one purpose of this book is to reveal God and Jesus Christ the Son of God; and to persuade people to let the word of Christ dwell in them richly, Col. 3. 16. I make no excuse for using the personal pronoun. This is a personal message. Think how often St. Paul uses the word "I". There are many personal experiences here. When the heart is full of a message and one longs to share his experiences, and the Bible truths he has learnt, nicety of language and carefully rounded phrases cannot be considered. "My heart was hot within me, while I was musing the fire burned: *then* spake I with my (PEN)", Psa. 39. 3.

May God richly bless the reader and the reading of this book.

THE UNKNOWN GOD

BY

One Who Loves Him

LONDON

PICKERING & INGLIS LTD.

Pickering & Inglis Ltd.
29 Ludgate Hill, London, E.C.4
229 Bothwell Street, Glasgow, C.2
59 Cross Street, Manchester, 2
5 Hope Way, Liverpool, 8
56 Grainger Street, Newcastle-upon-Tyne
29 George IV Bridge, Edinburgh, 1
Loizeaux Bros., 19 West 21st Street, New York
Home Evangel, 418 Church Street, Toronto 2

BOOK
PRODUCTION
WAR ECONOMY
STANDARD

THIS BOOK IS PRODUCED
IN COMPLETE CONFORMITY
WITH THE AUTHORIZED
ECONOMY STANDARDS

Made and Printed in Great Britain

Contents

CHAPTER I

Our God Unknown

FORTY years ago, at my first visit to Keswick Convention, G. H. C. MacGregor, one of God's saints, said: "What hinders a fully-satisfied life is *want of knowledge*—knowledge of GOD". Then he added: "I remember what dear Andrew Murray, that great Bible student, once said to me, as he looked into my eyes with a gaze one can never forget, 'My brother, the trouble with us Christians is, WE DON'T KNOW OUR GOD'." Some months ago I remembered that remark, coming from such a gifted exponent of Scripture, and it startled me greatly—more deeply than I can ever tell. I knew my Bible; but did I know *God*? On my knees the cry went up to God, "O Lord, reveal to me my own ignorance of Thee, and its remedy".

May every reader of this incident ask himself: "What do *I* know of God?" His promises, His goodness, kindness, graciousness, forgiveness, warnings, condemnations, and power? What do I know of His LOVE? Of His PEACE? Of His JOY? Of His GLORY? Being laid aside recently through ill-health, and suffering great bodily pain, that remark, "We DON'T KNOW OUR GOD", came to me as a direct and definite personal challenge. Then and there I made up my mind that my chief aim in life should be to *know God*: to gain from the Scriptures a real and full knowledge of my Saviour, as far as it was possible for me, especially of GOD'S GREAT LOVE for us; for after all, "God is LOVE".

7

How few of us realise the great importance, yea, the vital importance of *knowing God*. Everything in the Christian life depends upon it. When our Lord, the night before His crucifixion, was in close communion with the Father, He said that He came to give eternal life; adding, "and this is life eternal that they might KNOW Thee, the only true God, and Jesus Christ, Whom Thou has sent", John 17. 3. But our Lord came, not only to give "life", but also the "more abundant" life, John 10. 10. This fuller life must come from fuller knowledge of God. Our Saviour came from the Father in order to manifest, reveal, *show* just what God is like. All His words and works had this object in view; so that He could say, "He that hath seen Me hath seen the Father", John 14. 9. When Philip said, "Shew us the Father", our Lord replied, "Hast thou not *known Me*, Philip? He that hath seen Me hath *seen* the Father".

Everything that God allows to befall us, is allowed for the one purpose that we may know more of Him. What we call disappointments are *His* appointments.

Is it not therefore quite clear that our purpose in life ought to be, so to live that in our words and deeds we may manifest the Saviour Who dwells in our hearts, so that others may desire to know Him? St. Paul was taught this great truth as *his very first lesson*. He heard a voice saying unto him, "Saul Saul, why persecutest thou Me?" And he said, "Who art Thou, Lord?" And the Lord said, "I am Jesus, Whom thou persecutest", Acts 9. 4. I wonder how soon Saul came really to *grasp* the truth that Christ dwells in the heart of every Christian man, woman, and child? But the great question for you and me to ask ourselves is this: Do *I* realise this truth, and all it means and all it involves? Listen to him once again: "I live; yet *not I*, but Christ liveth in me: and the life which I now live in the flesh *I live by the faith of the Son of God*, Who loved me, and gave Himself for me", Gal. 2. 20. My belief is that St. Paul was persecuted, and underwent more suffering for his Master's sake than any other man who ever lived. But even in his afflictions he saw God's dealings with him, and realised his Saviour's foreknowledge. During those three days of blindness, he prayed for guidance. Then came regained sight; and Christ's plan—promise!—for him, was given to Ananias. "I will shew him how great things he must SUFFER for My Name's sake." Was ever such a "commission" given to any other man? Yet all through his years of unparalleled suffering, he was always rejoicing, and bidding others to "rejoice in the Lord". When he spake of his afflictions he would add, "I therein do rejoice, yea, and will rejoice. . . . Christ shall be magnified in my body (made magnificent, made to be seen great) . . . For to me to live is CHRIST", Phil. 1. 18-21. "God hath shined IN (not only into) our hearts, to give the light of the KNOWLEDGE of the glory of God in the face of Jesus Christ . . . that the LIFE also of Jesus might be made manifest in our body", 2 Cor. 4. 6-10. Do we possess such "knowledge"? If Christ, the Light of the World, dwells in our hearts in full possession, we shall not even wish to put up any "black-out" there. If we do so wish, we need not trouble—for there will not be much light to hide.

One who has recently been called to higher service, once said, "How many of us, I wonder, have realised that there is only one Person in the wide universe who can live the Christian life, and that is the Lord Jesus Christ Himself?" It is His life. We can no more live His life apart from the fact that He indwells us, than we ourselves can live anybody else's life. The Christian life is essentially the OUTLIVING of the INLIVING Christ. "Christ liveth in me." A little girl reading her Bible aloud said this: "that whosoever believeth in Him should not perish but have 'internal' life". How true! When we believe in Him, the Lord Jesus actually lives within us, and so enables us to live the life we should live.

The greatest lesson that you and I can learn, is that God has put us into this world for the *sole purpose* of our being "to the praise of the glory of His grace". "He hath chosen us in Him (Christ Jesus) . . . that we should be holy and without blame before Him in love", Eph. 1. 4-6. And the indwelling Christ alone can enable us to be this. Moreover, we must *"know* Him Whom we have believed". So St. Paul prays "That He would grant you according to the riches of His GLORY; to be strengthened with might by His Spirit in the inner man; that Christ may *dwell in your hearts* by faith; that ye being rooted and grounded in love, may be able to comprehend with all saints what is the breadth, and length, and depth, and height; and to KNOW the love of Christ which passeth knowledge, that ye might be filled with all the fulness of God", Eph. 3. 16-19. Note that this is not merely for "the elect few": it is for *"all* saints", that is, *all* believers. How many of us know very much even *about* "God's great love wherewith He loved us", and still loves us? Eph. 2. 4. How many of us KNOW that love by personal experience?

"I count all things but loss for the excellency of the KNOWLEDGE of Christ Jesus my Lord: for Whom I have suffered the loss of all things . . . that I may win Christ, and be found in Him, not having mine own righteousness . . . but that which is through the faith of Christ, the righteousness which is of God by faith: that I may KNOW Him, and the power of His resurrection", Phil. 3. 8-10. "My life abides in heaven" is one translation of Phil. 3. 20. Think of "Jesus Christ: Who is gone into heaven, and is on the right hand of God; angels . . . being made subject unto Him", 1 Pet. 3. 22. But we also are taught to pray that we may do His will on earth as the angels do it in heaven.

Prayer: Lord Jesus, make me and keep me "subject unto" Thee.

> "Father, I know that all my life
>   Is portioned out for me;
> And the changes that are sure to come
>   I do not fear to see.
> But I ask Thee for a present mind,
>   Intent on serving Thee."

> "The LOVE of Jesus, what it is,
>   None but His loved ones know."

It is quite possible that quite a number who are reading this book are saying to themselves: "Yes, but these are the experiences of great saints; men mightily used of God; men always in the eye of the public and swaying multitudes. But *I* am living a very humdrum life with little opportunity of influencing others. I have not the incentives Paul had: nor have I his opportunities of witnessing for my Saviour.

To such we would reply: Read the last two verses of the Acts of the Apostles. There we hear of another side of the apostle's witness for the Master. "And Paul dwelt two whole years in his own hired house, and received all that came in unto him, preaching the kingdom of God, and teaching those things which concern the Lord Jesus Christ, with all confidence, no man forbidding him." Is not that *your* opportunity?

A friend said to me: "I called to see —— recently. He sent you his love. I found him in the kitchen talking with an ice-cream man, whom he had just led to accept Christ as his Saviour."

CHAPTER II

Our Ideas of God

A BRILLIANT young authoress asked Dr. Jowett, the famous Master of Balliol College, Oxford, a searching question: "Dr. Jowett, what do you think of God?" He turned and gazed at her with an earnest look, then quietly replied, "Young lady, it matters very little what *I* think about God; but it matters very much what God thinks about *me*". As an undergraduate at Oxford in those days, that struck me as a very clever and wise reply. But now I see that Professor Jowett was wrong. *It matters very much* what a man thinks about God. To every one of us, our thoughts about God are of supreme importance. In fact, many people who regard themselves as Christians never give God a thought from morn till eve; although they would much resent being classed with the wicked man of whom it is said: "God is not in all his thoughts", Psa. 10. 4.

Is not God largely unknown to us who really love Him and desire to serve Him? Forgive me for being intensely personal and laying bare my own soul. In my early years the 119th Psalm was a great rebuke to me. The feeling produced in my mind was that King David far outstripped me in his delight in the Word of God. He would cry, "O how love I Thy law!" v. 97. "Thy law is my *delight*", v. 77. Then there came a time when it was possible for me to say: "In His Law do I meditate day and night", Psa. 1. 2. But my meditations were almost entirely on my own relationship to God—*how* to pray; *how* to live a holy life; *how* to live a victorious life.

People knew me as a Bible student. One great evangelist, much used by God, actually said to me recently: "You know your Bible better than anyone I know". Two or three years ago such a remark would have caused me much joy. But to-day it merely arouses a feeling of real sorrow; for *now* I see that it is *knowledge of God* that is the greatest possession anyone can have and enjoy: "Whom to KNOW is life eternal". (See John 17. 3). It is impossible to express in words the intense joy—"joy unspeakable and full of glory"—which filled and flooded the heart, when the Bible came to be to me just *a revelation of God's love*. No one can truly be said to KNOW God unless he *knows* "the love of Christ which passeth knowledge", Eph. 3. 19. True love withholds nothing that is good from the object of its love. It yearns and longs to be able to give even more than its resources can supply. But God the Father "loveth the Son and hath given all things into His hand", John 3. 35—the hand that gives; and we know that the earth is "full of His riches", Psa. 104. 24. Moreover we are bidden to trust "in the living God Who giveth us *richly* all things to enjoy", 1 Tim. 6. 17. Then are we not told that "the same Lord over all, is rich unto ALL that call upon Him"? Rom. 10. 12. How much do we "call upon Him" for? Well may the Psalmist bid us to "taste and *see* that the Lord is good": "they that seek the Lord shall not want any good thing", Psa. 34. 8, 10. "*No* good thing will He withhold from them that walk uprightly", Psa. 84. 11. Yet how is it that so few true Christian people live and act as though they really believed this? Our hearts assure us this is true of our God. It seems to me that if we really KNEW God, and knew His promises, *and truly believed that He means what He says*, our lives would be always and absolutely full of joy and rejoicing. One thing would happen: we should ask for much more than we do ask. Doubt and worry and anxiety, would—not flee away,

—but *cease to trouble us*. All the "happenings" in our lives would be just the "All things" that "work together for good" to us who love God, Rom. 8. 28. Then our friends and acquaintances would come to class us with those that "looked unto Him and were RADIANT: and their faces were not ashamed", Psa. 34. 5, Amer. R.V.

But we cannot live such carefree, joyous lives, just because we *know* these things. Only love can bring forth love in return. So our greatest aim in life should be to learn and to KNOW that "God *is* love", by learning the ways in which He has revealed His love to us. The Bible is given to us expressly for this very purpose. "All Scripture is given by inspiration of God and is profitable for doctrine, for reproof, for correction, for instruction in righteousness: that the man of God may be PERFECT, throughly furnished unto all good works", 2 Tim. 3. 16, 17. Even in the Old Testament we find men of great holiness. For example, who among us has risen to such saintliness, passionate devotion, and earnest outspoken witness for God, as David? Yet he was truly a man very subject to "like passions as we are": passions which once led him into very grave sins. But when forgiven, God restored unto him "the joy of salvation", and *upheld him* with His free spirit; and he became a man after God's own heart. Psa. 51. 12. But in the Old Testament we read of great saints who were at times despondent and impatient— sometimes bitter and unbelieving. Even Elijah prayed, "It is enough; now, O Lord, take away my life", 1 Kings 19. 4. And Jeremiah cried, "O Lord, revenge me of my persecutors", 15. 15. There is nothing like this in the New Testament. It is a remarkable fact that in all the records of distress, and persecution, and great tribulation, there is not a word of discontent or complaint. Think of St. Paul's unparalleled sufferings. Read the list in 2 Cor. 11. 23-33. Labours, stripes, prisons, beatings, scourgings, shipwrecks, and numberless perils. Yet there is never a word or a hint of discontent or complaint; nothing but a glorying in them. "Who shall separate us from the love of Christ?" he cries exultantly: "shall tribulation, or distress, or persecution, famine, nakedness, peril, sword? Nay, in all these things we are more than conquerors through Him that loved us", Rom. 8. 35-39. "We glory in tribulations . . . because the *love of God* is shed abroad in our hearts by the Holy Ghost", Rom. 5. 3-5. The same loving spirit is revealed by St. John. Even Simon Peter and his obscure and despised converts could manifest a love for Jesus Christ that gave them 'joy unspeakable and full of GLORY,' 1 Pet. 1. 8. Now, why are these things so rare in us to-day? Why are there so few truly radiant Christians? Do *you* know *any* such?

A lady whom I know, told me that as she passed by a Church in a London suburb one Sunday, a working man said to his companion, "Look at 'em, Bill! I've seen a hundred or two people go in there and not a single *smile* among 'em!" No, the worldling calls us "kill-joys". So we would ask this most important question: Can we discover the secret of the joy and radiance of those early Christians in the first century? Is it possible to re-capture it—to possess it? Most surely it *is* possible, since it *all* comes from our blessed Saviour, "Jesus Christ", Who is "the same yesterday, and to-day, and for ever", Heb. 13. 8. In our gratitude to Him for all the goodness and patience He has shown to us, we ought, at *least*, to be willing to look into these things. Believe me, all our Christian work, all our preaching, all our personal witness is of little value unless we have such love to Him that it gives us "joy unspeakable and full of GLORY". We have often thought how easy it was for those early disciples who lived *with* our Lord, to live entirely *for* Him. We used to sing as children, and still join in such hymns, which declare, "I wish that His hands had been placed on my head". "I should like to have been with

Him then". But even in the inner circle of our Lord's disciples—His apostles—there were quarrels, and disputes as to who should be greatest, and a seeking of seats on His right hand and on His left in His kingdom. Sometimes they even contradicted their Master. Once "Peter took Him, and began to rebuke Him, saying, Be it far from Thee, Lord: this shall not be unto Thee", Matt. 16. 22. James and John wished to call down fire from heaven upon those who would not receive their Lord! Luke 9. 54. They even forbade a man to cast out devils, v. 49. And at the last, Simon Peter nearly killed a man among those who came to arrest our Lord. And when the Saviour needed their loving fellowship most, they all forsook Him and fled; and, with the solitary exception of St. John, *they left Him to die alone.*

Then there came a miraculous change in those men. They gladly and rejoicingly endured bitter opposition, persecution, imprisonments and martyrdom. They and their converts lived such radiantly happy lives; and their words and deeds were so wonderful that the heathen thought they were gods "come down . . . in the likeness of men", Acts 14. 11, 12. But the most amazing thing, humanly speaking, is that those disciples did greater works than the works done by the Saviour Himself! John 14. 12. We know, of course, that those works were done by Christ Himself dwelling in them. It was "the Lord working with them, and confirming the word with signs following", Mark 16. 20. Again we ask: Why? What is the secret of all this instantaneous change in those disciples? It is of the greatest importance to us that we should find the answer to such a question, because you and I are meant to go and do likewise. WE are included in Christ's promise. In fact the promise was given to us! Our Lord said, "He that believeth on ME, the works that I do shall he do also; and greater works than these shall he do: because I go to the Father",

John 14. 12. Our primary duty, then, is to discover the secret of such a life of power, of joy, and of love.

But you may say: Oh, *such things* do not happen to-day. A few Christian workers, and whole-time evangelists, were talking over this question, when one of them, turning to me, asked, "You travel about very much all over the country. Do *you* ever meet truly radiant Christians?" My thoughts at once went back to a rare saint of God doing twenty years in Sing Sing convict prison for a desperate crime. I paid a visit to the prison simply to meet that truly delightful *saint*. What won this hardened criminal for Christ? Simply the discovery of John 3. 16: "God so LOVED the world, that He gave His only begotten Son, that whosoever believeth in Him should not perish, but have everlasting life". *Christ's infinite love* won him; and his was, without doubt, joy unspeakable and full of GLORY. After thirty minutes' fellowship with him, the Governor came in. Pointing to my newly-found friend, he turned to me and said: "That man is the greatest power for good in this prison". Then he turned to the prisoner and said: "You can't go far wrong here, but will you be able to stand when you get out?" "Will I *stand*?" he cried. "No, not I, but my Saviour will be able to hold me up."

CHAPTER III

Joy Unspeakable

ON my last visit to Keswick, a year or two ago, another striking thing happened. Arriving by the Keswick special train from Euston, I made my way at once to the house of my kind hostess. A youth of some twenty-three years of age stood on the doorstep. He told me that he was alone in the house: all the others were at the station. He had never been to Keswick before, so I suggested climbing Castle Head to see the view. He was an Afrikander who had recently come to England to study for the ministry. After a little chat about the coming convention, I begged him to tell me how he came to know Christ as his personal Saviour. And this was his story.

My home is in Bloemfontein. Our farm was five miles away from our nearest neighbour, and twenty miles from the nearest town. When fourteen years of age a Christian lady said to me, "I am disappointed in you. I thought you would be a minister". I made no reply. The time came for me to leave school, and father asked whether I would join him on our farm, or go into business. I had been taught to read a verse or two out of the Bible each day, and was a nominal Christian. At this juncture I chanced to read part of the first chapter of 1 Peter, and verse 8 arrested my attention: "Jesus Christ, Whom having not seen, ye love; in Whom, though now ye see Him not, yet believing, ye rejoice with JOY UNSPEAKABLE, and full of GLORY". Until that moment I *thought* I was a Christian, but never had such a great joy, as St. Peter tells of, come to *me*. Joy unspeakable! I would do anything to get such joy. For some weeks I agonised in prayer, pleading for "joy". But unspeakable joy did not come. In despair I turned to God, calling upon Him to *save* me; and He did so, and *with Him came* JOY—"the joy of the Lord". So *now* I am training for the ministry.

As we made our way to Friar's Crag, we met a man who was doubtful whither a certain pathway led, and at my suggestion he came with us. The question was put to him, "How did you come to know Christ as your personal Saviour?" He gladly told me *his* story. It was this:

I come from Egypt. My father, a Copt, had become a Christian, and because of that I regarded myself as one. I considered myself a "good boy", and when old enough, started preaching the Gospel and doing other Christian work. Was I not a "good boy"? One day, in my Bible reading, I came upon a verse in 1 Peter 1, which spoke of "Jesus Christ, Whom having not seen, ye LOVE; in Whom, though now ye see Him not, yet believing, ye rejoice with JOY unspeakable, and full of GLORY". So I asked myself: Why have not *I* such joy? I am *a good boy* and deserve to have it. So I prayed earnestly for two or three months, always with the thought, I'm a *good boy*. Then God convicted me of sin. At last I threw up my hands in despair, and cried: "O God I am lost, and I thought I was so good. Save me". The moment I took the place of a *lost sinner*, Christ found me. I remembered then that He said, "The Son of Man is come to seek and to save that which was lost", Luke 19. 10—so He came to seek and to save *me*. Then and there I at once dedicated my life entirely to God's service.

Is it surprising that the strange similarity of the experiences of those two men—one from South Africa and the other from the North, gave me much food for thought, and much questioning as to the depth of my own love for

Christ Jesus. Mine was a joyous life, but never had *joy unspeakable* been my lot. Why not? The fact that the Lord Jesus had actually *sent* a man hundreds of miles from North Africa; and another a few thousand miles from South Africa to impress upon me that there was, in His gift, "joy unspeakable and full of glory" impressed me deeply. My meeting those two total strangers in one brief half-an-hour revealed God's great love and compassion for *me*. And God is taking the same interest and care and trouble with every one of His children.

But there—a Convention is a very busy time, and the matter was shelved. Months afterwards sickness became my lot, accompanied with very great physical pain; and it was *in this* that the "joy unspeakable and full of glory" became a reality to me. Do you ask, "How"? Its roots are in LOVE—love to Christ. But how can we learn to love Christ more deeply? Surely only by getting to know more of God's love to us. Love springs from *Knowledge*. "We love Him because He first loved us", 1 John 4. 19. St. John, the apostle whom Christ Jesus specially loved, writes: "We have KNOWN and BELIEVED the love that God hath to us. God is love, and he that dwelleth in love dwelleth in God, and God in him. Herein is our love made perfect", 1 John 4. 16, 17. Yet I had never studied my Bible to find out *how greatly Jesus loves us*. What a sad confession to make! At once the resolution was made that henceforth all my time should be spent on studying the Word of God—the God Who IS LOVE—in order to KNOW the greatness of His infinite love; and to pass on to others by lip and by pen, and by *life*, the knowledge of His great love.

St. John says: "We know that the Son of God is come, and hath given us an understanding that we may KNOW Him that is true, and we are in Him that is true, even in His Son Jesus Christ", 1 John 5. 20.

May the Holy Spirit inspire every reader of these words

to seek to *know* Him, Whom to know is life eternal; and then by life and by lip, and by look, reveal to others around us the amazing love of Christ Jesus. He is counting on *us*.

One of the saddest—nay, the very saddest lament our Lord uttered was in His cry to the Father, near the end of His earthly life. Read it again, and put in a little word which occurs in the Greek, but is omitted in our English translation. Scholars say it cannot easily be translated. It *needs* no translation—its agony is only too obvious. Read it first in your Bible, John 17. 25: "O righteous Father, the world hath not known Thee." Now let us add the "untranslated" word, and finish the verse:

"O righteous Father—AND the world hath *not known* Thee! But I have *known* Thee: and these (His disciples) have *known* that Thou hast sent Me".

Then our Lord discloses the secret and source of our love to God by which alone comes joy unspeakable and full of glory. "And I have declared unto them Thy name"—*i.e.* Thy nature, Thy character, *Thyself*—"and will declare it: that the LOVE wherewith Thou hast loved Me may be in them, and I in them", v. 26.

Do try to get a clear grasp of that wonderful utterance. God the Father's infinite love *may* be *in* you and *in* me, just as Christ dwells in our hearts by faith. What is His purpose there? It is this: "That ye, being rooted and grounded in LOVE, may be able to comprehend with all saints what is the breadth, and length, and depth, and height; and to KNOW the love of Christ which passeth knowledge, that ye might be filled with all the fulness of God. . . . Unto Him be glory", Eph. 3. 17-21. What manner of men we ought to be! What manner of men we *may* be, may become, if only we are "filled with all the fulness of God". Yet most of us are content with reading, with a delightful thrill, the wonderful things St. Paul prays for on behalf of his converts, Eph. 3. 14; and then to go on our way without claiming or seeking this inestimable gift of God.

My earnest desire is to urge all my readers to follow the example of the angelic host: for do we not pray daily, "Thy will be done in earth, as it is in heaven", Matt. 6. 10.   Immediately after writing about loving Jesus Christ "with joy unspeakable and full of glory", St. Peter tells of "the sufferings of Christ and the GLORY that should follow"; then adds, "which things the angels desire to look into", 1 Pet. 1. 11, 12.   Yet how few of us seem to have any such desire!   May the Holy Spirit testify to *us*, *constrain us*, and lead us into such a love for our Saviour that it gives us joy unspeakable and full of GLORY.

"How greatly Jesus must have loved me!
How greatly Jesus must have loved me!
To bear my sins, to bear my sins
In His body on the tree."

"Changed from Glory into glory,
    Till in heaven we take our place;
Till we cast our crowns before Thee,
    Lost in wonder, love, and praise."

CHAPTER IV

The Greatness of God's Love

HAVE you ever given even ten minutes to think over God's love to us? Is it possible to love people whom we do not know? If we know *about* them we may have a respect and even an affection for them, yet not *love* them. But when we reflect upon love to God it is possible to say, "Whom having not seen we *love*", because He reveals Himself in our hearts by faith. And the more we know about His love, the more we are likely to love Him. "For He is altogether lovely . . . and this is my Friend", Song of Solomon 5. 16. St. Paul prayed that his converts might be able to comprehend with ALL saints what is . . . the LENGTH of God's love. The highest of all revelations is to have God revealed unto us that we may know how much He loves us; so that we may have a complete assurance of that love, and fully trust His love. *Our* love for people often waxes and wanes. God's love is unchangeable. Jesus Christ is "the same yesterday, to-day, and for ever", Heb. 13. 8. *He* never varies. Long before our Lord came to dwell on earth, God said to His people: "I have loved thee with an everlasting love: therefore with lovingkindness have I *drawn thee*", Jer. 31. 3. Can you fathom the meaning of everlasting love? Or can we resist the amazing wonder of such love? It passes our imagination that anyone can refuse or wound such love; yet, at times, all of us are guilty of doing so. Let us think over this everlasting love, the greatest thing that can occupy our minds.

(1) When did it BEGIN? What was the commencement

of it? There must have been a time when God formed the earth on which we dwell. Now God loved us, His people, *before that*. Before man was made, God in His infinite foreknowledge had us individually in His mind, and had formed His plans for us. It is absolutely beyond our comprehension; but it is part of God's foreknowledge of the future. We must confine ourselves to facts revealed in the Scriptures. *When* did His love for *me* begin? The inspired Word reads thus: "Blessed be the God and Father of our Lord Jesus Christ, Who hath blessed us with all spiritual blessings . . . according as He hath chosen us in Him *before the foundation of the world*": that is, this earth on which we dwell. It was created specially for *man. You* were in the mind of Christ in those ages long ago! *I* was in His mind then. But He chose us for a purpose: "that we should be holy and without blame before Him *in love*", Eph. 1. 3, 4. (Are we?) There never was a time when God did not love His people.

(2) When will this love CEASE? It will never cease, nor decrease; it is an everlasting, never-changing love. All through eternity, God will pour out His love upon us. We are told that "When He shall appear, we shall be like Him; for we shall see Him as He is", 1 John 3. 2.

What will take place during "those ages to come"? The Scriptures reveal a little. "God Who is rich in mercy, for His great love wherewith he loved us, even when we were dead in sins, hath quickened us together with Christ, and hath raised us up together and made us sit together in heavenly places in Christ Jesus: that *in the ages to come* He might shew the exceeding riches of His grace in His kindness toward us through Christ Jesus", Eph. 2. 4-7. And we shall "know even as also we are known", 1 Cor. 13. 12. Not that we shall know Him as *fully* as He knows us; but we shall know Him in the *same manner* as He knows us; His thoughts will be our thoughts, and our thoughts always His thoughts. In a new way we shall "know the things that are freely given us of God", and in a fuller way we shall realise that "we have the mind of Christ", 1 Cor. 2. 9-16. But, blessed be God, we shall LOVE Him even as also He loves us, because then there will be nothing in us to oppose or grieve His love. The love our Lord prayed for on our behalf then will be love fully appropriated by us: "that the LOVE", said our Lord to the Father, "wherewith Thou hast loved Me, may be in them, and I in them", John 17. 26.

(3) Let us, however, never forget that this love may be received now, here on earth—be realised *here*, just in so far as we *trust* His love for us. Listen! Since the beginning of the world men have not heard, not perceived by the ear, neither hath the eye seen, O God, beside Thee, what Thou hast prepared for him that waiteth for Him, Isa. 64. 4. St. Paul quotes that verse with a suggestive alteration and addition. He says, "for them that LOVE Him"; adding "but God *hath revealed them unto us* by His Spirit". "Now we have received . . . the Spirit which is of God; that we might KNOW the things that are freely given to us of God", 1 Cor. 2. 9-12. Surely every child of God ought to have an earnest desire to *know* these things? The Holy Spirit *glorifies* the Saviour, when He "takes" of Christ, "receives" of Christ's "things"— words or deeds—and "declares" or "shows" them unto us, John 16. 14, A.V. and R.V. Shall we not look to the Holy Spirit to do this for us; and *listen* to Him? For everything Christ said or did was a revelation of God's love.

Scholars tell us that the literal translation of the reply to His mother given by the Lord Jesus and recorded in St. Luke 2. 49, is, "Wist ye not that I must be in the *things* of My Father?" All His works and words were a revelation of God the Father. "He that hath seen Me", said our Lord, "hath seen the Father", John 14. 9. Our Lord desires everyone who believes on Him to reveal the indwelling Christ to others around us, just as He revealed the Father. How important it is then to *know* Him Whom we have believed, 2 Tim. 1. 12. This is more than just knowing facts *about* Him. The brothers of the Saviour knew Him intimately in the home-life for some thirty years. They lived with Him, yet they did not believe *on* Him till after His resurrection. We read in John 7. 5, "neither did His brethren believe on Him". St. Peter says, "Unto you therefore which believe He is precious", 1 Pet. 2. 7, and we usually love to show to others our precious things. If we only *knew* it, the Lord Jesus is the most precious of all.

But it is not only our friends that "take knowledge" of us that we have "been with Jesus", and that His spirit is revealed in us, Acts 4. 13; but even the hosts of angels and archangels learn lessons from us. We might have thought that it was enough for them to have the Risen and Glorified Saviour back in their midst. What wonderful *new* things they could learn from Him. But the Holy Spirit revealed to St. Paul that they also learn from *us*—from you and from me—things about God and His love, which they could not learn from the glorified Saviour direct, or from the other angels!

Listen to this: "Unto me, who am less than the least of all saints is this grace given, that I should preach . . . the unsearchable riches of Christ; and to make all men see what is the fellowship. . . . To the intent that NOW unto principalities and powers (angels) in heavenly places might be made known by the *church* (*i.e.* true believers of *all* denominations) the manifold wisdom of God", Eph. 3. 8-10. It is no wonder that St. Peter writes, "which things the angels desire to look into", 1 Pet. 1. 12. But the angels desire only the things which God tells them to desire. *What* things is St. Peter thinking of? Just the power of God which keeps us, v. 5; the trial of the believers' faith; our love, and our "joy unspeakable and full of glory"; and the salvation of our souls, 1 Pet. 1. 5-9.

Is it indeed really possible that angels can learn from you and from *me*, some new way of witnessing for Christ, and ministering to the needs of others? For "are *they* not all ministering spirits sent forth to minister for them who shall be heirs of salvation?" *i.e.* for you and me, Heb. 1. 14. "We also are compassed about with so great a cloud of witnesses." But we do not look to *them*. We "run the race looking unto Jesus", Heb. 12. 1, 2.

Is it not an utterly astonishing thing that any believer on Christ as His Saviour should seldom give much thought to these things, and rarely, if ever, trouble to look into them? At the close of day, the question often arises in my mind, "How much has the angelic host learned "of the manifold wisdom of God", by watching *me* and my walk to-day"? St. Paul prayed for his converts, that "He would grant you, according to the riches of HIS GLORY . . . That Christ may dwell in your hearts by faith; that ye being rooted and grounded in love may be able to comprehend with ALL saints what is the breadth, and length, and depth, and height, and to *know* the love of God that passeth knowledge, that (*in order that*) ye might be filled with all the fulness of God", Eph. 3. 16-19. What an amazing prayer! Yet the apostle adds, "Now unto Him that is able to do exceedingly abundantly *above all that we ask or think*, according to the power that worketh in us, unto Him be glory in the church by Christ Jesus, world without end", Eph. 3. 20-21. That is, perhaps, the most wonderful of all the prayers of St. Paul. *Do we* know enough about God's love to "comprehend" these things? There can be no joy like that which comes from being filled with ALL the FULNESS OF GOD. Pray much over the thoughts which the apostle gives us. God's love:

(1) Its BREADTH. The Psalmist said, "Thy commandment is exceeding broad", 119. 96. God's love for you,

and for me is broader. "If ye love Me keep My com-
ments", said our Lord, John 14. 15. The breadth of
God's love for us men is wide as the whole world. "God
so loved the WORLD that He gave His only begotten Son,
that whosoever believeth in Him should not perish, but
have everlasting life", John 3. 16.

> "For the love of God is broader
> Than the measure of man's mind,
> And the heart of the Eternal
> Is most wonderfully kind."

(2) Its LENGTH is eternal, everlasting; for God is everlasting life, Gen 21. 33; Isa. 40. 28; Rom. 16, 26; and
gives us everlasting JOY, Isa. 35. 10; 51. 11; 61. 7. Let
us repeat God's message to Jeremiah: "I have loved
thee with an everlasting love; therefore with lovingkindness have I drawn thee", Jer. 31. 3.

(3) Its DEPTH. How deeply the Lord Jesus feels for
our sorrows and grieves over our sins! Jeremiah cried,
"Behold and see if there be any sorrow like unto my
sorrow"—the sorrow of the Saviour, Lam. 1. 12. For
He not only "bare our sins in His own body on the tree",
1 Pet. 2. 24; but "He hath borne our griefs and carried
our sorrows", Isa. 53. 4. Yet let us never forget that
underneath are the everlasting arms, Deut. 33. 27.

(4) Its HEIGHT. This is quite beyond our imagination.
We can only sing with the angelic host, "Glory to God
in the highest", Luke 2. 14. And "neither height, nor
depth, nor any other creature shall be able to separate
us from the love of God which is in Christ Jesus our
Lord", Rom. 8. 39. Wherever we are, God's love is
there.

May we all long to *know our God* more fully—to know
Him and the power of His resurrection, Phil. 3. 10; and
to share His "joy unspeakable and full of glory". And
with our yearning desire let us couple a diligent searching
of the Scriptures—the greatest revelation of God's love.

"The Lord hath been mindful of us; *He will bless us,*" Psa. 115. 12.

"And can it be, amid revolving worlds,
  Our little world has been in God's great thought?
Mindful of us? So that His hand upholds,
  And for our good has loved and planned and wrought?

"Mindful of us—our nation? Higher still,
  Of us His Church; our family, of us?
Of you and me? O let the blest thought thrill!
  Mindful of us, to save us from sin's curse.

"Mindful of us, amid the mighty throng;
  Mindful of us through all the days now past;
And with brave spirits we may raise our song,
  He will be mindful, long as life shall last."

WILLIAM LUFF.

Let us never forget, however, that merely to *know* things about God is not enough. Do the terrible words of warning uttered by St. Paul apply to any of us? "They are without excuse: because that when they KNEW God they glorified Him not as GOD, neither were thankful; but became vain in their imaginations, and their foolish heart was darkened. Professing themselves wise, they became fools", Rom. 1. 20-22.

CHAPTER V

God is Love

THE secret of a life of power is an unshaken conviction that God is love, and can do nothing contrary to His infinite love. Since the Cross is the greatest revelation of God's love for man, it was impossible for His first disciples to realise and know how great the love of Christ is until His crucifixion and resurrection were accomplished.

There may be no *need* for me to dwell upon the truth of the foregoing statement, but it is one of such great importance, that we must recollect what the Holy Spirit says in the Scriptures concerning it. "Hereby *perceive we* the love of God, because He laid down His life for us", 1 John 3. 16. "In this *was manifested* the love of God towards us, because that God sent His only begotten Son into the world, that we might live through Him. Herein is love, not that we loved God, but that He loved us, and sent His Son to be the propitiation for our sins", 1 John 4. 9-10. "For God so loved the world that He gave His only begotten Son (to 'be lifted up' on the Cross, v. 14) that whosoever believeth in Him should not perish, but have everlasting life", John 3. 16.

Do we truly believe *in* Him and *on* Him (R.V.)? It is not enough for us merely to be baptized with *water* and be "received into the Church". It is not enough to *know* a great deal *about* the love of God for us. Each of us must have a personal *trust* in Jesus Christ as our personal Saviour, Who loves us so much as to die for us.

St. John confesses, "We have known and *believed* the love that God has to us. God is love, and he that dwelleth in love dwelleth in God, and God in Him", 1 John 4. 16. Evidently some of the converts of St. John were not *sure* of their conversion or their salvation. For he writes: "These things have I written *unto you that believe* on the name of the Son of God; that ye may *know* that ye have eternal life", 1 John 5. 13.

Just as the *Cross* was the greatest revelation of God's love, so the resurrection of the Lord Jesus from the dead is the greatest revelation of God's power to save us from the *punishment* of sin, and from the *power* of sin over us, in our daily walk and work.

The Saviour not only "bare our sins in His own body on the tree, that we being dead to *sins*, should live unto righteousness", 1 Pet. 2. 24; but He also "ever liveth to make intercession" for us; "wherefore He is able to save them to the UTTERMOST that come unto God by Him", Heb. 7. 25. St. Peter says, "by Whose stripes ye were healed", 1 Pet. 2. 24. The Lord Jesus dwells within us, "for the perfecting of the saints, for the work of the ministry", Eph. 4. 12—ministering to those around us. "Let us go on unto perfection", Heb. 6. 1. This does not mean *"sinless* perfection", but growth into maturity of godliness.

Now the greatest incentive to holiness, and the greatest transforming motive for it, comes from a knowledge of the amazing love of Christ for us. It is of this "great love" that we greatly desire to write.

In an earlier chapter we saw that God's love is everlasting. "His great love wherewith He loved us" had no beginning, it is eternal. "He hath chosen us in Him (the Lord Jesus Christ) before the foundation of the *world*, that we should be holy and without blame before

Him in love", Eph. 1. 4. Note that word "WORLD"—
it means our earth; not the millions of "worlds" in space.

"In the beginning God created the *heaven*." It is only
in these last days that we are beginning to understand
the vastness of that creative act.

Sir Arthur Eddington, one of our greatest astronomers,
recently declared that there is enough matter in the
universe to make stars as big as our sun to the number of
1, followed by 22 noughts! There are 100,000 million
stars in a galaxy; and 100 thousand million galaxies!
He added that astronomers believe our SUN to be *exceptional among stars*; and our earth to be absolutely
exceptional among planets. Are you beginning to ask
yourself: "What has this to do with the love of God?"
Just this. God chose us in Him (Christ Jesus) "BEFORE
the foundation of the world", Eph. 1. 4—our world, *i.e.*
this earth. He had already "created the heaven", which
included our sun, which is absolutely unique among suns.
Where should He place man? There was a heavenly
communing among the blessed Trinity, when God said,
"Let US make man in our own image, after our likeness. . . . So God created man . . . in the image of God created
He him", Gen. 1. 26, 27. He had chosen to do this *before*
the foundation of the *earth*, Eph. 1. 4; but in God's loving
purpose none of the millions of planets was good enough
for us, so He made our unique earth for our abode.

Scientists tell us that our earth came out of the sun,
because, for one reason, there is nothing in this planet
of ours which does not exist in the sun.

We are "sons of God." *That* is also unique. "Unto
which of the angels said He at any time, Thou art My
Son"? Heb. 1. 5. Unto *none* of them. Sons of God!
"Heirs of God and joint-heirs with Christ . . . that we may
be also glorified together," Rom. 8. 17. Glorified together
with Christ! "The things which God hath prepared for
them that love Him", 1 Cor. 2. 9. But sin came in to mar

the beauty of this world. Thorns and thistles sprang up, and all who love the Lord Jesus "desire a better country, that is a heavenly; wherefore God was not ashamed to be called their God: for He hath PREPARED for them a city"— even heaven itself, Heb. 11. 16; another revelation of God's love.

But heaven is prepared for children of God. Have you the assurance that you *are* a son of God?

Now there is another time when God lifted the veil, as it were, and allowed us once more to hear the communion together of the blessed Trinity. It is a very remarkable passage of Scripture; for in it we are allowed to share the meditations of God Himself. Just think of it! It was as though God the Father invited anyone to tell Him how a sinner—a repentant sinner—could find his way back to God: how the thing could possibly be done. "I am *willing*, tell me how?" My heart goes out toward the wanderers. But none in heaven or earth could answer the question. So God answers His own question, He had said, "How shall I put thee" (My people who are so rebellious) "among the children"? And God said, "Thou shalt call Me FATHER; and shalt not turn away from Me", Jer. 3. 19.

That is the way back to God. "Father, I have sinned against heaven, and before Thee, and am no more worthy to be called Thy son", Luke 15. 18, 19. The Father's great love even for a prodigal is shown by his joyous words to the servants, and again to the elder brother, "This my son was dead, and is alive again; and was lost and is found", verses 24 and 32.

And what does *our* loving Father expect from those who *are* His children? Surely, *at least* a love for others who have wandered from Him, whom He still loves dearly. So the next time we see the veil lifted and get

a vision of the unseen world, we learn how God yearns
for prodigals to return to Him through the ministry of
those of us who *are* children of God, sons of God. It is
in His dealings with the prophet Isaiah. He is a prophet
especially dear to us. But a time came in his life when he
seemes to have drifted away from holy things. So God
gives him a wonderful vision. The prophet tells us about
it in chapter 6 of his prophecy. He says, "I saw also the
Lord sitting upon a throne, high and lifted up. . . . Above
it stood the seraphims. . . . And one cried to another and
said, Holy, holy, holy is the Lord of hosts: the whole
earth is full of His GLORY. . . . Then said I, Woe is me,
for I am undone; because I am a man of unclean lips . . .
for mine eyes have seen the King, the Lord of hosts.
Then flew one of the seraphims unto me, having a live
coal in his hand . . . and he laid it upon my mouth, and
said, Lo, this hath touched thy lips; and thine iniquity
is taken away, and thy sin purged". Cleansed lips!
The only sin of which we can imagine Isaiah to have
been convicted is that of unwillingness to witness for
God to a sinful people. Unclean lips cannot witness
effectively to God's holiness.

But notice that the moment he confessed his sin,
immediately there came forgiveness and cleansing.
And then he heard the voice of the Lord saying: "Whom
shall I send, and who will go for Us?" Then said Isaiah,
"Here am I: send me!" And God said, "Go".

We are *all* sent into the world to be witnesses for God.
Ours are the only lips God has to use for that purpose.
In all our intercourse with one another there should be
a graciousness, a kindliness which makes others think
of God. The Lord Jesus Himself says to *us*, "Go". It
was one of His last commands. "Go ye into all the world",
said He, "and preach the Gospel to every creature",
Mark 16. 15. Now, we cannot *all* be foreign missionaries;

some of us must stay at home. However, there are some
millions of God's creatures in England, or U.S.A., or
Australia. Wherever *you* live you will meet them. God
wants us to witness for Him in every way and every day.

We may never walk to preach anywhere, but we can
always preach as we walk. The learned and "pious"
"elders and scribes" saw Peter and John in Jerusalem
after Christ's resurrection and heard them speak, and
"perceived that they were unlearned and ignorant men".
But "they marvelled" at them, "and they took knowledge of them that they had been with JESUS", Acts 4. 13.
You and I ought earnestly to desire and seek to make it
obvious to those whom we meet, that we have "been
with Jesus" and that Jesus is always with us.

God has sent to us, not "one of the seraphims", but
His dearly beloved Son to purify our hearts, and to
cleanse our lips, and to speak through those lips to others.
It was when our Lord Jesus Christ gave the command
to His disciples to go into all the world and teach all
nations, that He also said: "All power is given unto Me
in heaven and in earth, . . . and lo, I am with you ALWAY"
—yes, and "even unto the end of the world". The command is for *us*: but so also is the promise of His presence
with us.

But there is another occasion where we are allowed to
overhear the most heart-stirring communion between
the Father and the Son. The record of it is given us in
St. John 17, the most sacred thing ever written, the
Holy of Holies of the Bible. In it we are allowed to hear
the Son of God talking with God the Father, recounting
the gifts the Father has bestowed upon Him, and telling
the Father how He has used those gifts, not only for the
blessing of His disciples there present, but for every one
of us who loves the Saviour. He prays for His disciples.
He prays for *you* and for *me*, v. 20; so that *the world* may

believe that He—the Lord Jesus—was sent by the Father. Verse 8 speaks of the disciples of Christ's day. Verses 20 and 21 speak of us.

In a following chapter we must dwell upon that. Our Lord said, *"Every one* that asketh receiveth; and he that seeketh findeth", Matt. 7. 8. My asking and seeking therefore have not been in vain.

We would earnestly beg of you, however, that you would note that one of our Saviour's earliest utterances was this: "Blessed are the pure in heart for they shall see God", Matt. 5. 8. So heart purity is possible for every believer, but it is possible *only in Christ*; and we must yield ourselves wholly and utterly unto Him if He is to have His way with us, and we are to do His will.

Heart purity is only possible when there is willing obedience to the promptings of the Holy Spirit on our part. Our Lord, Who did "always those things that please" the Father, could say at the end of His earthly life as Son of Man, "I have finished the work which Thou gavest Me to do", John 17. 4. We *know* what that work is. "He came to give His life a ransom for many". He came "to seek and save the lost". He came that we "might have life", and "have it more abundantly", John 10. 10. He came to leave us an example that we might follow His steps, 1 Peter 2. 21: that is, "going about doing good", Acts 10. 38.

But He assures us, "I am the Way"; and it is possible only to "as many as received Him, to them gave He power to become sons of God, even to them that believe on His name", John 1. 12. "I AM THE WAY, THE TRUTH, AND THE LIFE", John 14. 6. Christ is the compass directing our path. Christ is the Truth, revealing all we need to know about God. Christ is the Life, the principle, the divine Being in us that lives. So that we can say, "For me to live *is Christ*", Phil. 1. 21. "I live, yet not I, but Christ liveth in me", Gal. 2. 20.

Now our Lord tells the Father *and us* what is His greatest desire for us: "I pray . . . that they all may be one: as Thou Father art in Me, and I in Thee, that they also may be one *in Us*: that the world may BELIEVE that Thou hast sent Me. . . . I in them, and Thou in Me, that they may be made perfect in one: that the world may KNOW that Thou hast sent Me; and hast loved them, as Thou hast loved Me . . . for Thou lovedst me before the foundation of the world", John 17. 21-24. These are some of the most wonderful words ever spoken. They reveal a most wonderful life that is possible for us.

Am I wrong in believing that if we only knew more of God's love for us we would come to love Him with joy unspeakable and full of glory? God is love—that is His name: that is His nature, His character, His very *being*. So our Saviour brings to an end this time of amazing communing with the Father, by telling Him, and us, the great and final purpose of His "coming" to earth: "I have declared unto them Thy Name, and WILL DECLARE IT: that the love wherewith Thou hast loved Me, may be IN THEM, and I IN THEM", John 17. 26.

CHAPTER VI

God Rising Early

THE love of God, like the peace of God, "passeth all understanding". We have seen this great love in the creation of our unique earth—so full of wonder. With what love and joy God planned it all! The very first page of Scripture breathes a spirit of love. We are told that at each step God expressed His joy. "Day" after "day", we read, that "God saw that it was good".

> "God made a *garden* first, I find,
> Another way of being kind;
> And the things we see in the garden grow,
> Are the words He has written to tell us so."

Then came that amazing revelation of LOVE. "God said, Let us make man in our image, after our likeness: and let them have dominion . . . over all the earth. . . . So God created man in His own image", Gen. 1. 26-27. The first object man saw was God Himself, and the first words man heard were the words of God *blessing him*, ver. 28. There stood a perfect man—radiant with the very glory of God. It was *then*, we are told, that "God saw every thing that He had made, and behold it was *very* good", verse 31. And when man became very *bad*, God still loved him, and never deserted him; and "men began to call upon the name of the Lord", 4. 26. "Enoch walked with God", 5. 22, 24. Yet after all this display of goodness and love, the earth became corrupt. The great flood came. It would appear that in a few years' time no God-fearing man existed, except the mysterious Melchizedek, Gen. 14. 18. But God did not

desert man. "The God of GLORY appeared unto Abram",
who must have lost faith in idols. Abram lived in the
"great flood" area, Acts 7. 2; and God became his "friend".
The great God of the universe would speak of him as
"Abraham My friend", Isa. 41. 8. And our Saviour
desires every child of God to be *His friend*. Did He not
say to His disciples, "Henceforth I call you not servants...
but I have called you friends: for all things that I have
heard of My Father I have made known unto you?"
John 15. 15. How it rejoiced the Saviour's heart to have
"friends". Do you not see the *love* in His heart? And, wonder of wonders, He desires *our* love; seeks our love, and
whispers to us living to-day: "Ye are My friends, if ye
do whatsoever I command you", John 15. 14. And
what *He* bids us do is always for our highest good and
greatest happiness and joy. In our heart of hearts we
know this; yet we are so slow to *believe* it and to trust
Him! and "What a Friend we have in Jesus!"

Have you ever considered how God honoured this
man who was the first to be called the "Friend of God"?
No man who ever lived has been so honoured. His name
is reverenced to-day the wide world over: by Christians,
by Jews, and by Moslems. It was *this* man who offered
to God the first *known* prayer, Gen. 15. 2, 3. How we
are tempted to envy him that privilege!

But we must remember that God has "no favourites".
His love is infinite and for all alike. Yet He sometimes
has to remind us, because of His great love for us, and
His yearning desire that we should always share His
joy, that any sin in the heart or life, prevents Him from
richly blessing us. Is He speaking to any of us to-day
these words: "Your sins have withholden good things
from you"? Jer. 5. 25. They always do so. How it pained
God's heart to say that! One of the saddest men I ever
met was a wealthy Colonel, who could not, *dare* not,
allow his only son more than thirty shillings a week,

because the son was such a hopeless drunkard. My heart bled for that father.

Believe me, God is waiting, longing to bless us and *make* us an untold blessing to others—with all the joy that this would give us—if only we were wholly yielded to Him, and did everything for love to Him and for His glory. When God chose a "blessing" for Aaron the high priest to give to His people, He chose the very best one possible. He always does. What was it? "The Lord bless thee, and keep thee: the Lord make His face to shine upon thee, and be gracious unto thee: the Lord lift up His countenance upon thee, and give thee peace", Num. 6. 24-26. The Lord's desire is to bless *us* also. But any allowed sin of thought or deed, or word, or act of disobedience, will hide from us the light of His countenance. On the last page of the Old Testament we read God's conditions for fulness of blessing—which is just another word for the outpouring of His love and Himself: "Bring ye all the tithes into the storehouse . . . and prove Me now herewith, saith the Lord of hosts, if I will not open you the windows of heaven, and pour you out a blessing, that there shall not be room enough to receive it", Mal. 3. 10. The "tithes" are an acknowledgment that all we have and are belong to God. When we truly *believe* this and act upon our belief, holding ourselves and all that God has given us, entirely at His disposal, we shall be so greatly blessed of God that the blessing will overflow to all around, because *we* have not room enough to take it all in, until we pass some of it on.

Can we not "trust . . . in the living God, Who giveth us richly all things to enjoy", 1 Tim. 6. 17? Or do we allow "the god of this world" to blind our minds? 2 Cor. 4. 4.

God made very great promises to His "friend" Abraham, but the greatest of all is recorded in Gen. 15. 1: "Fear not Abram: I am thy shield and thy exceeding great reward". Could there be any greater reward? "The Lord thy God . . . is mighty; He will save, He will rejoice over thee with joy; *He will rest in His love,* He will joy over thee in singing", Zeph. 3. 17. The literal translation of the Hebrew of the words in italics is, "He planneth silently in love". We need never be sorry for any disappointment, or illness, or loss—unless it be because of our *sin*. Sorrow and joy are not close friends. The Divine command is: "Neither be ye sorry; for the JOY OF THE LORD is your strength", Neh. 8. 10. The word "strength" means "stronghold". "The name of the Lord is a strong tower: the righteous runneth into it, and is safe", Prov. 18. 10.

If we knew more of the thousands of God's promises revealed in the Scriptures, our lives would always be very full of joy. For remember that it is still true to-day that "There failed not ought of any good thing which the Lord had spoken unto the House of Israel: all came to pass", Josh. 21. 45. "They that seek the Lord shall not *want* any good thing", Psa. 34. 10. We cease to *want* it because we *have* it. "The Lord is a sun and shield: The Lord will give grace and GLORY: no good thing will He withhold from them that walk uprightly", Psa. 84. 11. Yet we need to be reminded again and again that God's word "standeth for ever". God hath said: "I will perform that good thing which I have promised", Jer. 33. 14.

Let us never forget that "It is a good thing to give thanks unto the Lord; and to sing praises unto Thy Name, O most High", Psa. 92. 1. *Think* on these things. "Thou wilt keep him in perfect peace whose mind is stayed on Thee: because he trusteth in Thee", Isa. 26. 3.

Perhaps there are some reading these lines who are in deep sorrow, or even shame, because of the sin or sins of which they have been guilty. But remember the way back to God by repentance and faith *is always open*.

Some of God's most wonderful tokens of *love* are oft-times bestowed upon just such people when they accept His salvation. God's chosen people had been scattered. The remainder would suffer sword, pestilence and famine. Yet God still declared His love for them; and His yearning desire to bless them. And He longs to do the same for any and every penitent sinner. What was God's message for them? "I will bring them again unto this place; and I will cause them to dwell safely; and they shall be My people, and I will be their God: and I will give them one heart . . . that they may fear Me for ever, for the GOOD of them. . . . I will not turn away from them, to do them good. . . . Yea, I will REJOICE over them, to do them good. . . . With MY WHOLE HEART and with MY WHOLE SOUL. . . . will I bring upon them all the good that I have promised them. . . . I will cleanse them from all their iniquity. . . . I will pardon all their iniquities. . . . And it shall be to Me a name of JOY, a praise and an honour before all the nations of the earth, which *shall hear all the good* that I do unto them. Again there shall be heard . . . the voice of joy and the voice of gladness. Praise the Lord of hosts; for the Lord is good. . . . I will perform that good thing which I have promised", Jer. 32. 37-42; 33. 8, 11, 14. "I will cure them, and will reveal unto them the abundance of peace and truth", 33. 6.

There seems to me that no greater proof of God's great love than this is to be found anywhere else in the Old Testament. We might indeed be constrained to cry aloud, "Who is a God like unto Thee, that pardoneth iniquity? . . . He retaineth not His anger for ever; because He delighteth in mercy. . . . He will have compassion on us", Micah 7. 18, 19.

We have said enough to prove God's love, and goodness, and yearning desire to bless us, and make us a blessing. Yet it is beyond the power of man to unfold all God's love in words. David must have felt this when he wrote the 107th Psalm. "O give thanks unto the Lord, for He is good: for His mercy endureth for ever. Let the redeemed of the Lord SAY SO", verses 1 and 2. Again and again he recounts God's mercies and blessings which came when men "cried unto the Lord". And again and again he exclaims, "Oh that men would praise the Lord for His goodness, and for His wonderful works to the children of men", verses 8, 15, 21, 31. By our *lips* we ought to acknowledge this; but our lives also ought to be an eloquent testimony of the gratitude we feel.

So far we have taken our proofs of God's love from the Old Testament. The New Testament Scriptures speak for themselves—they just breathe the love of God for us: its breadth, and length, and depth, and height. It "passeth knowledge". And to *know* that love is to be "filled with all the fulness of God", Eph. 3. 18, 19. And when we are *filled* with the love of God, no one can come in contact with us without some of that love flowing over them. Yes, and if they jar or jolt us a bit roughly, the greater will be the love that o'erflows. Forgive a homely illustration, but do not forget it. And remember that the more the "overflow" of the love of God, the *fuller* we shall be.

> "Oh fill me with Thy fulness, Lord,
> Until my very heart o'erflow
> In loving deed and kindling word,
> Thy love to tell, Thy praise to show."

Bishop Taylor Smith was visiting a man in an East London hospital, and on his way to his bedside he passed a nurse carrying a glass of milk to a thirsty patient. Stopping her, he said, "Nurse, you are doing a great work. Are you doing it wholly for the glory of God?" "Yes, Bishop—*in a way*—but I find it very difficult with unreasonable and bad-tempered patients. They get on

my nerves." The Bishop said gently, "My dear young
lady, *that's* your opportunity! *There* is your chance of
revealing God's great love. What's that in your hand?"
"A glass of milk." "Now, if I jolt into you, what will
come out of that glass?" Laughingly she replied, "Why,
milk, of course!" "Yes", said the Bishop, "and every
time men 'jolt' you in a grumbling, grousing manner, if
you are filled with love for God, LOVE will come out—
God's love; and you will be a spiritual blessing to a needy
soul".

GOD RISING UP EARLY

It is deeply impressive, and very touching, to find God
using human figures of speech to compel us to come to
know how much He loves us. Jeremiah, who is sometimes called a gloomy prophet, was actually led by the
Holy Spirit to picture God rising up early in the morning
to send His messages of loving invitation: "Obey My
voice", Jer. 11. 7; 7. 13; 7. 25; 25. 3, 4; 29. 19.

For more than ten years the prophet pictured God
"rising up early and speaking"; rising up early and
sending. Eleven times over is this figure of speech used
in Jeremiah. And God will never cease pleading with
us. He even promised His stubborn and rebellious people
that in seventy years' time He would still come to them
and draw them into the folds of His love. "For I know
the thoughts that I think toward you, saith the Lord:
thoughts of peace, and not of evil. . . . Then shall ye call
upon Me, and ye shall go and pray unto Me, and *I will
hearken unto you.* And ye shall seek Me, and find Me,
when ye shall search for Me with all your heart. And I
will be found of you", Jer. 29. 11-14.

Listen to His promise: "Open thy mouth wide and I
will fill it. But My people would not hearken to My
voice: and Israel would none of Me", Psa. 81. 10, 11.
But you and I do not rebel to such an extent. Yet all

of us are tempted to believe that we must not go "all out" for God.

Yet the promise still stands: "The Lord God is a sun and shield: the Lord will give grace and GLORY; *no good thing* will He withhold from them that walk uprightly", Psa. 84. 11. We must get to *know* God better if we are to trust Him fully. Does not God say: "Let him that glorieth glory in this, that He understandeth and KNOWETH Me, that I am the Lord which exercise lovingkindness, judgment, and righteousness in the earth: for in these things I delight, saith the Lord", Jer. 9. 24. We must not misunderstand that bold figure of speech which God put into the mind of Jeremiah. The prophet does not say that God will wake up early in the morning; but that God will *rise* up. He that keepeth THEE will not slumber. "He that keepeth Israel shall neither slumber nor sleep. The Lord is thy keeper. . . . The Lord shall preserve thee from all evil; He shall preserve Thy soul. The Lord shall preserve thy going out and thy coming in . . . even for evermore", Psa. 121. 3-8.

We can rely upon God's "rising up"; but can He rely upon us? When we awake in the morning is our first thought of HIM? Do we wake early enough for a "morning watch"? It is no credit to me, nor do I say it in a boastful spirit—but the most wonderful messages from God are given me between five and six in the morning— the very moment I awake. That verse in Psa. 119. 18 is made very real to me *literally*: *"Open Thou mine eyes, that I may behold wondrous things out of Thy law"*. Morning after morning this happens, and pencil and paper are at once sought in order to write these thoughts down, and at the earliest opportunity they are told to others.

Is it because my last thoughts at night are given to God? The Psalmist evidently did this, for does he not

say, "How precious also are Thy thoughts unto me, O
God! . . . When I am awake I am still with Thee", Psa.
139. 17, 18. The Hebrew word used here for "thoughts"
means *will, desire*. It is used in verse 2: "O Lord, Thou
hast searched and known me. . . . Thou understandest
my *thought* afar off", Psa. 139. 1, 2.

The late John McNeill, one of God's great saints, tells
how deeply impressed he was when quite a small boy.
He would hear his father go downstairs in the early
morning as he fared forth to his work. "I would wait
breathlessly, as I heard the latch of the front door lifted,
and in the pause that followed, his voice was always
heard to say:

> "Forth in Thy Name, O Lord, I go,
> My daily labour to pursue,
> Thee, only Thee, resolved to know,
> In all I say, and think, and do."

Yes, it is still as true to-day, as in the days of Isaiah:
"Thou wilt keep him in perfect peace whose mind is
stayed on Thee", Isa. 26. 3.

That early morning acknowledgment of God so impressed little John McNeill that it influenced him all
his life.

CHAPTER VII

Joy in God

THERE are two things which astonish me very much.
The first is this, that in the Old Testament days the
saints of God were the possessors of such great joy. The
second surprise is that joy seems to be the last thing
which people to-day expect to find in "religion". "Your
commandments are a bundle of 'thou shalt nots'," is a
remark made to me by outsiders, not once nor twice.
Religion is regarded as a "kill-joy". If only Christian
people would buy a concordance, and look up every
Scripture which speaks of JOY, I believe it would make a
profound impression.

Will you read over, and pray over, just a few of the
Old Testament songs of JOY?

Nehemiah said: "The joy of the Lord is your strength",
Neh. 8. 10.

The Psalmist sings: "I will go unto God my exceeding
joy", Psa. 43. 4. "In Thy presence there is fulness of
joy", Psa. 16. 11. In these days, after the outpouring of
the Holy Spirit, we are not only in God's presence, but
"Christ dwells in our hearts by faith". We may therefore be, and *should* be, "filled with all the fulness of God",
Eph. 3. 17-19. If *that* does not bring us joy—abiding
joy, and joy that remains—I cannot conceive of anything
that would cause us "joy unspeakable".

The impression abroad to-day is that rich people are
less joyous than those who have little of this world's
goods. But it need not be so.

The "preacher" of very early Old Testament times says: "It is good and comely for one to eat and drink, and to enjoy the good of all his labour that he taketh under the sun all the days of his life which God giveth him. Every man to whom God hath given riches and wealth, and hath given him power to eat thereof . . . and to rejoice in his labour; this is the gift of God. . . . God answereth him in the JOY of his heart", Eccles. 5. 18-20. Note the words "labour" and "riches and wealth" *given by God*. Not the idle rich. Not those who become rich by profiteering, greed, and graft.

Of those who trust God fully and can say, "God is my salvation: I will trust and not be afraid: for the Lord Jehovah is my strength and my song: He is become my salvation," it is declared: "Therefore with joy shall ye draw water out of the wells of salvation", Isa. 12. 2, 3. Those who walk "the way of holiness" shall go with "songs and everlasting joy upon their heads", Isa. 35. 8. 10. "They shall obtain JOY and gladness; and sorrow and mourning shall flee away", Isa. 51. 11. "Everlasting JOY shall be unto them", Isa. 61. 7; "My servants shall sing for joy of heart," Isa. 65. 14. ."Be ye glad and rejoice for ever in that which I create: for behold I create Jerusalem a rejoicing, and her people a JOY. And I will rejoice in Jerusalem, and JOY in My people", Isa. 65. 18, 19.

"Thy word was unto me the JOY of mine heart", Jer. 15. 16. What *is* that "word"?

"I will cause them to dwell safely; and they shall be My people, and I will be their God; and I will give them one heart and one way . . . for the good of them . . . I will not turn away from them to do them good, but I will put My fear (reverent love) in their hearts. Yea, I will rejoice over them to do them good . . . with My whole heart and with My whole soul . . . so *will I bring upon them all the good that I have promised them*", Jer. 32. 37-42.

"Call upon Me and I will answer thee, and shew thee great and mighty things, which thou knowest not", Jer. 33. 3.

"Behold I will bring . . . health and cure . . . and will reveal unto them the abundance of peace and truth", ver. 6.

"I will cleanse them from all their iniquity . . . and I will pardon all their iniquities. And (they) shall be to Me a name of JOY, a praise and an honour before all the nations of the earth, which shall hear *all the good* that I do unto them: and they shall fear and tremble for *all the good* and for all the prosperity that I procure unto it", Jer. 33. 8, 9.

"There shall be heard . . . the voice of JOY and the voice of gladness . . . the voice of them that shall say, Praise the Lord of hosts: for the Lord is good . . . for His mercy endureth for ever", Jer. 33. 10, 11.

"Behold . . . I will perform that good thing which I have promised", Jer. 33. 14.

God *always* fulfils His promises: and He expects us to do the same with our promises and vows to Him.

"The Lord our righteousness", Jer. 33. 16.

Let us remember that these great and mighty and wonderful promises are made to those who fully trust Him. They were revealed to the man to whom people refer as "the gloomy prophet". He was by no means gloomy! What is to be our reaction to them? Surely our reply should be a complete and whole-hearted surrender to the will of God for us. A full trust that He is able to perform, and willing to perform, and earnestly longs to perform, all these good things on our behalf. Let us not keep back anything from Him. Then He will keep back no good from us. Let us not hold on to *any sin*—even sins of thought. Why are we so slow, so loth to yield ourselves wholly into His loving hands?

4

"The meek shall increase their JOY in the Lord",
Isa. 29. 19.

The Lord Jesus Who said:

"I am meek and lowly in heart", Matt. 11. 29.

"The Lord Thy God in the midst of thee is mighty:
He will save, He will REJOICE over thee WITH JOY, He
will rest (or plan silently) in His love. He will JOY over
thee with singing", Zeph. 3. 17.

"Enter ye into the JOY of the Lord", Matt. 25. 21, 23.

It would take up too much space to recount the loud
notes of praise which echo and re-echo through the
Psalms. Look at them; listen to them for yourself, and
mark the passages which show the source of the Psalmist's
joy. His great secret source was referred to by St. Peter
on the day of Pentecost:

"I foresaw the Lord *always before my face*, for He is
on my right hand THAT I should not be moved: therefore
did my heart rejoice and my *tongue* was glad", Acts
2. 25-26.

David himself said: "My heart is glad and my GLORY
rejoiceth".

Our tongue is one great factor in our GLORY.

"The kingdom of God is . . . righteousness, and peace,
and JOY in the Holy Ghost", Rom. 14. 17.

"The fruit of the Spirit is love, JOY, and peace",
Gal. 5. 22.

THE JOY OF THE LORD JESUS

If we seek joy—and who does not?—we ought to go
to the source of all JOY, *i.e.* the Lord Jesus Himself.
St. Paul said, "We have the mind of Christ", 1 Cor. 2. 16.

"Let this mind be in you which was also in Christ Jesus",
Phil. 2. 5.

The mind of Christ was always possessed by a deep
and joyous calm. The "Man of Sorrows" was always
full of joy; and we have already noted that He desires

His joy to be in us so that our joy "may be full". If our Lord's joy *is* in any one of us, it *must* overflow to others, because of its abundance.

(1) What things made the Lord Jesus rejoice?

When the seventy disciples returned from their preaching tour "with JOY", because of their welcome and fruitfulness, "Jesus rejoiced in spirit".

And every success of ours in our ministry should rejoice our hearts, because it rejoices the heart of Christ Jesus. The seventy had gone forth telling that the Messiah had come; and would come to them soon. See Luke 10. 1. But what a far greater message *we* have to proclaim by life, and look, and lip!

"In that hour Jesus rejoiced in spirit, and said, I thank Thee Father, Lord of heaven and earth, that Thou hast hid these things from the wise and prudent and hast revealed them unto babes; even so, Father, for so it seemed good in Thy sight", Luke 10. 21.

Those seventy disciples had never been so happy before; and the Saviour rejoiced over *their* joy and their success; which was due to their great delight in doing the Lord's will. Their joy was *pure*, because they gave the Saviour the credit for their success. "Even the devils are subject to us through THY NAME", Luke 10. 17. They did not try to pilfer God's glory. Christ told them that the secret of their greatest joy should be that their "names are written in heaven", ver. 20.

(2) What manner of JOY was Christ's?

(*a*) It was not just "being pleased" as we say. Nor was it only physical or mental joy. "Jesus rejoiced in spirit." The R.V. says, "He rejoiced in the Holy Ghost", Luke 10. 21, *i.e. by* the Holy Ghost, as the marginal reading gives it, verse 21. "The fruit of the Spirit is . . . JOY." As the peace of God "passeth all understanding", so does the the JOY of God.

(*b*) Christ's joy was a joy over the success of others.

Do we—you and I—ever give Christ joy; and give the angels of heaven joy, by casting out, in Christ's name and power and promises, devils of strong drink, passion, cruelty, and vice? cp. Luke 15. 10.

(c) *It was a humble joy*. He gave His Heavenly Father the credit of the success of the seventy. Perhaps God could give us *all* greater success in our witness, if it would not tempt us to take the credit of it to ourselves. The Saviour clearly hinted that great success in Christian work is not because the workers are "wise and prudent", but because they are mere "babes", doing what they were told to do. May God raise up more "babes"!

When we reflect upon the joy of the Lord Jesus, do we *never* ask ourselves (what seems to be the *obvious* thing to ask): "What shall I render unto God for all His benefits toward me"? Psa. 116. 12. Most of us are so eager to repay the kindnesses shown to us by our friends. Have we *no gratitude* toward the Saviour?

The Psalmist asked himself: "What can I do?" Then he gave the answer: "I will take the cup of salvation and call upon the name of the Lord", ver. 13.

That is a thing we can all do, and *ought* to do. Most of our readers *have* done this. But do we ever think of taking the cup of salvation to other people? Our friends, our acquaintances, and "heathen" at home and abroad? For, as we have seen above, *that* is one of the things that bring joy to the heart of our Saviour; and the angels of heaven who rejoice "over one sinner that repenteth."

So many Christians form their views of Christ from the crucifix. Many think of Him only as "a man of sorrows and acquainted with grief". Now we must never belittle the Cross. St. Paul, one of the most joyous of men, cried, "God forbid that I should glory, save in the Cross of our Lord Jesus Christ", but he gives his reason: "by

Whom the world is crucified unto me, and I unto the world", Gal. 6. 14.

Thank God that Christ "bare our sins in His own body upon the tree". The Saviour's name is often on the lips of the angelic hosts; and the name they sing of, and praise most, is "The Lamb". The Lamb that was slain.

But let us ever bear in mind that the Lord Jesus was the most joyous man who ever lived. At His birth the angels sang the "Good tidings of great joy". Did not the Virgin Mary cry, "My soul doth magnify the Lord: and my spirit hath rejoiced in God my Saviour"? and every time we sing those words we ought to be thrilled with joyful thanksgiving. When the Baptist saw Christ, he said, "This my JOY . . . is fulfilled", John 3. 29.

You must have noticed in the Gospel story that it was only the *religious* people who stood gloomily aloof, or heckled the Saviour when He spoke. "The common people heard Him GLADLY", Mark 12. 37. Our Lord often went happily to social gatherings; and the only time we read of His inviting Himself to a house, we find that it was to a publican's house, *i.e.* the house of a hated tax-gatherer, who received Him joyfully. The Saviour found pleasure and joy in all the works of God—birds and flowers, the bright sunshine which shone forth on the evil as well as on the good. He even likened Himself to a Bridegroom—the man of supreme happiness. The Lord carried happiness and joy with Him wherever He went. Even when He came face to face with the Cross, His words had a joyous ring about them; and He prayed that HIS JOY might be in all His followers.

What a joyous ring there was in His talks—we hesitate to call them "sermons".

Some may say: "Yes, it is all very well *talking* about joy; but if *you* lived with the people *I* have to live with you would sing a different song!"

But the "contradiction of sinners" never disturbed our Saviour's joy. Before our Lord left this earth—*i.e.* before His visible form left it—He said: "I will see you again and your heart shall rejoice, and YOUR JOY NO MAN TAKETH FROM YOU", John 16. 22.

Therefore, "Rejoice evermore".

In one part of India the Maharajah has proclaimed that all who go forth to draw water from a well in any part of his country, must go with a song on their lips—and go singing all the way. The reason for this command is that a man was found dying of thirst within a few yards of a well. *He did not know the well was there.* He never recovered consciousness.

And now, if you hear songs on the lips of one walking through the jungle to-day, you know that there is a well nearby.

The prophet Isaiah seems almost to have foreseen this when he cried: "The wilderness and the solitary place shall be glad for them; and the desert shall rejoice, and blossom as the rose. . . . Strengthen ye the weak hands, and confirm the feeble knees. Say to them that are of a fearful heart, BE STRONG, fear not: behold your God will come . . . even God. . . . He will come and save you . . . and an highway shall be there, and a way, and it shall be called The way of holiness . . . and the parched ground shall become a pool, and the thirsty land springs of water . . . and the ransomed of the Lord shall return and come to Zion with SONGS and everlasting JOY upon their heads; they shall obtain JOY and GLADNESS, and sorrow and sighing shall flee away", Isa. 35. 1-10.

The Lord Jesus wants His followers to be full of joy, and *always* full. And He has made every provision for this. Do you live with grumbling and complaining people? Well, *they* are just the ones that need joyous companions most. Some few years ago a lady wrote me rather an indignant letter from the South of France. This is how it ran: "It is all very well for *you* to write, as you do, about being always full of joy. If you were in my place you would soon alter your opinion. I am out here with my invalid mother. She is bedridden. *Nothing I do pleases her*, although I wait on her 'hand and foot'; but I can do nothing right. Never a word of thanks, but just grumble, grumble, grumble. But *perhaps* you know of a remedy"? My reply was just a reminder of Christ's love and promises, and power to keep us under all conditions. "Whatsoever ye do, do all to the GLORY of GOD." No answer was forthcoming. Some months later, while waiting in the speakers' room of a London hall, before the chairman led the way to the platform, the committee-room door opened and a lady in heavy mourning asked for me. She shook my hand warmly and said: "I am the sister of Miss —— to whom you wrote some time back. She consecrated her life to the service of our dear invalid mother, who recently passed away; and she did so for Christ's sake. She asked me to tell you that ever since your letter came she served mother *with positive joy.*"

Yes, the Lord Jesus is "able to save to the uttermost", Heb. 7. 25.

CHAPTER VIII

The Source of Joy

"JOY unspeakable and full of glory." It was *that* which arrested my attention. If only it might grip yours! There it is in Simon Peter's letter to his converts—spoken of as a common and natural possession of those early Christians! It existed *then*, but have you met anyone to-day who possesses such joy unspeakable and unshakable?

The great majority of those who read this book will be members of one Church or another; and probably a few have had the courage to invite their friends to join them in worship, but only if they can add with some enthusiasm: "Our Vicar, or Pastor, is *such* a good preacher". But the man of the world who is warming himself by jazz is not attracted by "sermons". Yet it is quite true that most worldlings have an idea that they must "get right with God" before they die, and that "religion" is some sort of insurance for heaven, which they believe to be an abode of bliss. But why *should* it be, if it is (to them) a kill-joy *here*?

Do you not think that the world at large thinks that church-going is the only thing that differentiates most Christians from non-Christians? At all events our churches are emptying, and picture palaces and dance-halls are crowded.

Now let me frankly confess that although my life had

hitherto been a very happy one, a great spiritual impetus
and uplift was given to it by meeting the Afrikander and
the Egyptian whose lives had been redeemed and made
radiant through that one verse of Scripture which told
of a "joy unspeakable and full of glory". In a moment
it was borne in upon me that this was the thing to attract
outsiders to the Saviour. But was such a joy *mine*?
Did I give evidence of it in my daily walk and occupation?
It was so *evident* that such a joy could come only from a
passionate love for the Saviour, and this in its turn could
only grow out of a deeper realisation of the fulness of the
greatness of *His* love for me. The Bible was suddenly
lit up by the love of God. *His* love now seemed to flash
forth from every page. It became a veritable love-letter
from the Heavenly Father to me, his child. Not merely
God's love, but a *Father's* love to *me*.

But "God so loved the world", and the world appre-
hends it not, comprehends it not. And the world will
never realise how God loves "the world" unless we
believers on the Saviour *reveal that love in our lives*, and
speak of it with our lips, and live and move as men and
women conscious of a Father's infinite love; confident
that His love is always choosing for us that which is
for our highest good and greatest joy.

The amazing "sense of joy" in those early Christians
to whom St. Peter wrote, was no doubt partly due to
their realisation of the things from which they had been
delivered by accepting Christ as their Saviour. Truly
they had come out of darkness into light, out of utter
degradation of body and soul to become possessors of
the unsearchable riches of Christ, Eph. 3. 8.

But we may perhaps never feel such an incentive.
What can we put in its place? We need not go beyond
the pages of Scripture to find out. Our Lord told us four
ways in which we may secure joy.

(1) ANSWERED PRAYER. But do you ever *look* for an answer? Yet think over our Lord's sevenfold promise on the eve before His Cross and passion.

(*a*) John 14. 13: "Whatsoever ye shall ask in My Name, that will I do, that the Father may be glorified in the Son"—the Lord Jesus, Who *dwells in our hearts by faith*: glorified *there*.

(*b*) John 14. 14: "If ye shall ask anything in My Name, I will do it."

(*c*) John 15. 7: "If ye abide in Me, and My words abide in you (*i.e.* obedience) ye shall ask what ye will, and it shall be done unto you."

(*d*) John 15. 16: "Ye have not chosen Me, but I have chosen you, that ye should go and bring forth fruit, and that your fruit should remain (abide): that whatsoever ye shall ask the Father in My Name, He may give it you."

(*e*) John 16. 23: "Verily, verily, I say unto you, Whatsoever ye shall ask the Father in My Name, He will give it you."

(*f*) John 16. 24: "Hitherto ye have asked nothing in My Name: *ask and ye shall receive* that your JOY may be full."

(*g*) John 16. 25, 27: "I shall shew you plainly of the Father. At that day ye shall ask in My Name; . . . for the Father Himself loveth you, because ye have loved Me, and have believed that I came out from God." "Be of good cheer (JOYFUL) I have overcome the world", verse 33.

Seven times He spake: "ASK", "RECEIVE", "JOY". Forgive another personal testimony. Since "joy unspeakable" laid hold of me as the greatest expression of God's love, I have been truly amazed at the way God answers prayer. In the most unexpected and most unlooked-for ways He sends the answer. One cannot here go into details. The fact remains that whenever there is a difficulty to be overcome, or a problem to be solved the way is made plain. In countless ways God's promise is fulfilled day after day. "It shall come to pass, that *before they call* I will answer; and while they are yet speaking I will hear", Isa. 65. 24. And these oft-repeated tokens of God's love and watchfulness are such evident proofs of His love, that joy fills the heart and *thrills the heart*.

Remember that His gifts are always greater than ours. He always does "exceeding abundantly above all we ask or think," Eph. 3. 20. Joy always comes from answered prayer.

(2) BIBLE STUDY. Every lover of the Lord Jesus must desire to know as much about Him as possible; and the Scriptures are a mine of information. Are we not bidden by our Lord to "search the Scriptures"? After our Lord had instituted the last supper, He gave the apostles the most wonderful talk that ever came from His lips. One object of that talk was that they should receive JOY unspeakable. Did He not *say* so? "These things have I spoken unto you, that MY JOY may be in you, and that your JOY may be fulfilled", John 15. 11, R.V.; or may *"be full"*, A.V. What were "these things"? Verses 10 and 12 tell us *two* of them: "If ye keep My commandments, ye shall abide in My love; even as I have kept My Father's commandments, and abide in His love", ver. 10. "This is My commandment, that ye love one another, as I have loved you", ver. 12. "Ye are My friends if ye do the things which I command you", ver. 14, R.V. Does not this make it perfectly plain, that our JOY cannot be full unless we *know* the things our Saviour bids us do? How many of us are Bible students? *Study especially* St. John, chapters 14 to 17.

Then we come to an amazing source of JOY:

(3) PERSECUTION. "Blessed are ye when men shall hate you, and when they shall separate you from their

company, and shall reproach you, and cast out your name as evil, for the Son of Man's sake. REJOICE ye in that day, and LEAP FOR JOY: for behold your reward is great in heaven", Luke 6. 22-23. How unexpected a source of joy!

Yet we shall be following His steps. "He is despised and rejected of men", Isa. 53. 3. "Who when He was reviled, reviled not again", 1 Pet. 2. 23. "Who shall separate us from the love of Christ? Shall tribulation, or distress, or persecution, . . . or peril, or sword? . . . Nay in all these things we are more than conquerors through Him that loved us. For I am persuaded, that neither death, nor life, nor angels, nor principalities, nor powers . . . nor any other creature shall be able to separate us from the love of God which is in Christ Jesus our Lord", Rom. 8. 35-39.

(4) WINNING OTHERS FOR THE SAVIOUR. This is a most fruitful and blessed source of joy. "I say unto you that likewise JOY shall be in heaven over one sinner that repenteth", Luke 15. 7. And every soul-winner knows how great is the joy we ourselves feel over that. It is a clear sign that we are being true followers of Christ.

Quite early in our Saviour's ministry He went down to the shores of Lake Galilee. Peter and Andrew were "casting a net into the sea". Christ said, "Follow Me and I *will make* you fishers of men. And they straightway left their nets and followed Him". They soon found James and John "mending their nets; and He called them. And they immediately left the ship and their father, and followed Him", Matt. 4. 18-22.

Every reader will probably remember that our Lord knew all these four men before, on the first day that John the Baptist cried, "Behold the Lamb of God which taketh away the sin of the world", John 1. 29. The very next day the Baptist was talking with Andrew and John, when he saw the Saviour walking by; he said again, "Behold the Lamb of God!" "And the two disciples heard him speak, and they followed Jesus . . . and abode with Him that day."

After that interview Andrew at once found Simon Peter and said, "We have found the Messias . . . the Christ". And he brought Peter "to Jesus", John 1. 29-42. And John evidently brought *his* brother James. Then our Lord "findeth Philip, and saith unto him, Follow Me. . . . Philip findeth Nathaniel". How quickly they became "fishers of men"! So when our Lord "would go forth into Galilee" these disciples went with Him, first of all (?) to the marriage in Cana, John 2. 1, 2. After "following" our Saviour they evidently returned to their fishing, while continuing as part-time companions of Christ. See Luke 5. There we read of the great catch of fishes, and Simon Peter's cry, "Depart from me, for I am a sinful man, O Lord". "And Jesus said unto Simon, Fear not, from henceforth thou shalt *catch* men." Then "they forsook ALL and followed Him", Luke 5. 11. Simon Peter went home and put away his "fisher's coat", which he did not use again till after the resurrection of our Lord, John 21. 7.

Then came the Saviour's third-time command to Simon Peter: "Follow Me": and again, "Follow thou Me", John 21. 19, 21. And we never hear of Peter's "fisher's coat" again. Was not that "coat" the one thing Simon Peter held on to? He had "forsaken all" to follow Christ—but still, he might have to go back to the old life. But after the Saviour had so lovingly dealt with him and his grievous denial with oaths and curses, and had drawn from his lips that threefold declaration, "Thou knowest that I love Thee", Peter became entirely yielded to the Master's will. "Lord, Thou knowest all things"—how I took Thee and rebuked Thee, and called forth Thy rebuke for me, Mark 8. 32; how I denied Thee with oaths and curses; and how Thou didst freely and frankly forgive me, and didst appear to me the first of all *men* to see Thee after Thy resurrection, 1 Cor. 15. 5. "Thou *knowest*"—this time a fresh Greek word meaning "perceivest". "Thou perceivest that I love Thee", John 21. 15-18. This is the reinstated backslider who became so devoted to His Saviour that he could lead his converts to love the Lord Jesus, Whom *they* had never seen, "with JOY unspeakable and full of glory".

Quietly dwell in meditation upon what the Holy Spirit can do with a man wholly and utterly yielded to His teaching, His leading, and His love, Rom. 15. 30.

He can glorify every part of our nature. Look at Simon Peter, a fisherman, well on in years—for he was probably the oldest man among the apostles: older perhaps than Christ Himself. He was the most difficult man of the twelve disciples to mould; and the only one who would contradict his Master, and tell Him what to do. Yet our Lord chose *him*, foreseeing the desertion and denial. And scholars to-day declare that Peter's first Epistle is one of the "finest examples of vigorous style" in the whole Scriptures. And it is Simon Peter, and not only the loving and lovable John, who possessed such infectious joy unspeakable and full of glory that he could praise his converts for possessing it.

Who did all this for Simon Peter? He probably never possessed even a small portion of the Old Testament Scriptures; and the Rabbis had cumbered their teaching with so much erroneous doctrine. Peter went to no College and studied at no University. He was of comparatively humble birth, and after leaving school, could not, as a fisherman, consort with literary men and scholars. Yet he became a profound theologian and wrote his wonderful letters. Truly he is a writer deeply taught of God. "Was there ever a greater theological lecture given than his first Epistle?" asks a modern scholar. How did it come about? He was taught of God—taught by living with, listening to, and watching the Saviour, for Whom he came to have such a deep love.

His epistles came from his innermost being. And here are we to-day, thrilled by his messages, inspired by his life and words. Ever bear in mind that he passed through a tragic spiritual experience, as is the case with many of us. It seemed to be an end of all spirituality and even religion itself for him.

Yet one loving, understanding look from the Saviour recalled to him his Lord's foreknowledge and foretelling of this threefold denial, and it broke him down. He "went out and wept bitterly", Luke 22. 62. Then when our risen Saviour sought him out on the resurrection day and told him that *He* understands and loves to forgive, Peter became the great saint we know him to be. "There is JOY in heaven over one sinner that repenteth", Luke 15. 7, 10; but what must have been the rejoicing there when Simon Peter repented! Peter declares with great joy the fact that the angels are interested in the *mysteries of man's salvation*. "Which things the angels desire to look into", 1 Pet. 1. 12. He himself claims that he "preached the Gospel with—*i.e. in* or *by*, R.V., marg.—the Holy Ghost sent down from heaven". His converts were "kept by the power of God through faith . . . wherein ye greatly rejoice", says Peter, 1 Pet. 1. 5, 6. It is just as true to-day that the salvation of man occupies the attention of the universe, and the very angels of heaven are ministering spirits to you and me. Do we ever give a thought to these wondrous truths?

We beg you not to overlook the fact that unless Peter and John practised what they preached they would not have dared to write as they did to their converts. Moreover, they could not have led their disciples into any "joy unspeakable" which they did not themselves possess. I am convinced of this, that the apostles could not have *retained* their "joy unspeakable" unless they spake of it to others; and unless it was patent—manifest—in their own lives. Anyone who tries to be a "secret disciple" is no use to God or man. "Woe is unto me if I preach not the Gospel", wrote Paul, 1 Cor. 9. 16. To-day you and I might well add, "Woe unto me, if I do not reveal to others the love of God and the joy of our Lord".

Chapter IX

Herein is Love

"GOD so loved." Those three words sum up the message from God Himself sent to us in the Holy Scriptures. "God so loved the world that He gave His only begotten Son, that whosoever believeth in Him should not perish, but have everlasting life", John 3. 16. It is an all-embracing love. Probably that one sentence has brought more blessing to men and women and little children than any other sentence ever spoken or written. God *actually loves every one of us* with a passionate devotion; not, indeed, because we deserve His love, but because we *need* it. We are told that "Christ also loved the Church", and gave Himself for it: the *Church* that consists of those who have responded to that love, and love the Saviour in return, whatever denomination they belong to. But St. Paul is not content even with this, for does he not say: "The Son of God, Who loved ME and gave Himself for *me*"? Gal. 2. 20. So the wide circle is narrowed down to include *"me"*.

In every human being God sees something lovable. What a difference it would make in our lives if we constantly bore in mind that greatest of all truths: "God *loves* me". Try it for *one day*. "Keep yourselves in the love of God"—of "Him" Who is able to keep you from falling"—from "stumbling", Jude 21 and 24

God's love. It is my firm belief that there is nothing *unsaid* in the Bible that could have been said to prove to us that God loves us with a deep tenderness. Do you reply: "Then why write anything else about it"? Simply because the Bible, to *most Christians*, is practically an unknown book: rarely ever read, and very seldom *studied devotionally*. The result is that God is practically an unknown God.

In these days of international hatred and strife, men doubt God's love, and constantly ask: "Why does God allow this suffering? Why doesn't He stop the war?" Others look at their own little circle and cry: "Why does God allow this sickness, this bereavement, this disappointment?" But did you ever stop to think that Christ Jesus Himself *suffered*—"the Just for the unjust, that He might bring us to God"? 1 Pet. 3. 18. Our Lord was "God manifest in the flesh", yet perfect Man. "Behold the MAN!" "A Man of sorrows and acquainted with grief", Isa. 53. 6. Do we not learn *here* that it was essential and necessary that God, when He became man, should suffer sorrow, grief and pain?

Our blessed Lord foresaw how this problem of pain would perplex men of all time, and did He not spend *hours* on the afternoon of His resurrection day in explaining to two obscure believers: "Thus it is written, and thus it behoved *Christ to suffer*"? Luke 24. 45, 46. We, too, hide "as it were our faces from Him", Isa. 53. 3. when we stumble at the sorrow and pain in the world.

Our Saviour evidently regarded that afternoon's conversation as of more importance than even appearing to His own mother and to the band of the apostles, an event which took place later in the day.

Ought we not gladly to welcome the possibility of being "made perfect through suffering"? "For it became Him, for Whom are all things, and by Whom are all things, *in bringing many sons unto* GLORY, to make the Captain of their salvation perfect through sufferings", Heb. 2. 10.

In his later years Paul fully realised why the Lord Jesus sent that strange message to him by Ananias: "He is a chosen vessel unto Me. . . . For I will shew him

how great things *he must suffer* for My Name's sake",
Acts 9. 15, 16.

How gladly St. Paul *welcomed* suffering. It was foretold by his Saviour: ordained by Him. So he gladly
cries: "That I may know HIM . . . and the fellowship of
His sufferings", Phil. 3. 10. Let *us* also rejoice if God
trusts us to suffer for Him. "For as the sufferings of
Christ abound in us, even so our consolation also abound-
eth by Christ." We shall be "comforted of God"—
"the Father of mercies, and the God of all comfort;
who comforteth us in ALL our tribulation, that we may
be able to comfort them who are in ANY trouble, by the
comfort wherewith we ourselves are comforted of God",
2 Cor. 1. 4, 5. When trouble or sorrow comes, ask yourself at once: "Now, whom can *I* comfort?"

Without any shadow of doubt Saul of Tarsus became
after his conversion the happiest and most joyous man
who ever lived. But if he had met with nothing but
praise and admiration from all around, and possessed
wealth and power, we would be the first to say that his
joy and rejoicing sprang from these. We believe, however, that no follower of the Lord Jesus ever suffered as
much as Paul; yet his joy abounded more and more.
Again we urge you to read 2 Cor. 11. 23-28. Then listen
to his rejoicing: "I count all things but loss for the
excellency of the *knowledge of Christ Jesus my Lord*: for
Whom I have suffered the loss of all things, and do count
them but refuse, THAT I MAY WIN CHRIST", Phil. 3. 8-10.

May we all be *trusted with sufferings*, if our Saviour can
be better glorified by them. Let us never forget that:

> "In every pang that rends the heart
> The Man of Sorrows hath a part."

Among the Old Testament saints, Job is an outstanding
example of a great sufferer, and he bore his sufferings with
amazing patience. He could see no reason why God
should deal with him thus.

But had he only known that God had chosen him and was trusting *him* to be a lesson-book to Satan himself, he would have felt himself highly honoured! "Hast thou considered My servant Job, that there is none like him in the earth, a perfect man"? Job 1. 8. Yet *he* was allowed to suffer the loss of everything except life itself. But "in all this Job sinned not, nor charged God foolishly"; 1. 22. Our Saviour was never so gracious, never so mighty, never so triumphant, as when He refused to save Himself from suffering the agonies of the Cross, so that He could save others.

Herein is love! My pocket Bible has 1276 pages. They are just a revelation of God's great love for man. But far and away the most wonderful and most blessed of the whole book is the 17th chapter of St. John: the Holiest of Holies. It occupies just *one page*, but it is the greatest utterance ever made. It is full of precious revelations of God's love to us. St. Paul might well have been thinking of this prayer of Christ's when he wrote: "Eye hath not seen, nor ear heard, neither hath entered into the heart of man, the things which God hath prepared for them that love Him. But God hath revealed them unto us by His Spirit: for the Spirit searcheth all things, yea, the deep things of God", 1 Cor. 2. 9-10. Then he goes on to add: "We have received . . . the Spirit which is of God; that we might know the things that are freely given us of God", ver. 12.

But quite apart from anything that is recorded in John 17, the utterance itself is a great revelation of the place you and I hold in the heart of Christ Jesus: for *we* are included, and the Saviour is also actually praying for *us*, ver. 20. On the very evening that our Lord was about to reveal to His three nearest disciples: "My soul is exceeding sorrowful, even unto death: tarry ye here, and watch with Me", Matt. 26. 38, He had been revealing precious things to the apostles. Then He lifted up His eyes to heaven, and said: "Father", John 17. 1. Well may we listen! It is the Son of God communing with God the Father. Yet our Saviour is not talking so much about Himself as about His wondrous love for His disciples, and recounting what great things He had done for them, and would continue to do in them and through them. He speaks of the greatest gifts that can possibly be made. We are indeed on holy ground.

Now what is this Divine communing about? The Son of God is not speaking about thrones and dominions: not about cherubim and seraphim, or angels and archangels, or prophets and priests; but about humble and lowly men and women who believe on Him; and of those in succeeding generations who should come to love Him. Why, that includes you and me! Now what does that reveal to us? Surely it is a revelation of the depth and intensity of the love that God the Father and the Lord Jesus have *for us*, and for all believers. Nothing ever written reveals God's love for us and reveals the heart of God himself as John 17. It tells us what Christ had done for His loved ones. It tells us what Christ desires to do for us. They and we are God's precious jewels, Mal. 3. 17. Listen to His own words: "I have manifested Thy name" —Thy nature, Thy character, Thine own Self—"unto the men which Thou gavest Me out of the world: Thine they were and Thou gavest them Me", ver. 6. You and I are gifts of God the Father to God the Son! What great value He places on us!

When our Lord was speaking, the men and women of whom He spake were chiefly poor people, and very humble folk—fishermen, peasants, wayfarers, beggar men, blind, and halt and lame whom He had healed and befriended.

Then our Saviour prays for most astonishing gifts for us. "Sanctify them through Thy truth," ver. 17.

Our Lord then declares that it will be through them and *through us* "that the world may believe", "and that the world may know" that He Himself was sent by the Father; "and hast *loved them*"—said our Lord—"as Thou hast loved Me", vers. 21 and 24. Do *we*, you and I, give that "belief"—that knowledge—to the world? Do our worldly friends really gain the impression that you and I *are confident that God loves us* as dearly as He loves His only begotten Son?

The fact is, we have no notion how much God loves us. We have very little idea how precious we are in His sight. St. Paul says He loves us "with a love which passeth knowledge"—with a love which never fails nor fades. But our Lord goes beyond that. He closes His sublime communing with His Father with this greatest of all of His promises: "I have declared unto them Thy NAME, and will declare it: that THE LOVE WHEREWITH THOU HAST LOVED ME, *may be in them*, and I IN THEM", 17. 26. How many of us can truthfully say with St. John, "that disciple whom Jesus loved" especially: "We have *known* and *believed* the LOVE that God hath to us"? "God is love; and he that dwelleth in LOVE dwelleth in God, and God in him", 1 John 4. 16.

Let us never rest until we see the wonder of this; and come fully to realise just what it means. How much do we even *know* about the love of Christ for us? When a lawyer asked Christ a question, "tempting Him", saying, "Master, which is the great commandment in the law?" our Saviour courteously replied, "Thou shalt love the Lord thy God with all thy heart, and with all thy soul, and with all thy *mind*. This is the first and great commandment", Matt. 22. 36-38. We find this commandment in Deut. 6. 5; but there the command is "with all thine heart and with all thy soul, and with all thy *might*". This is *very significant*. Our Lord adds, "AND WITH ALL THY MIND"—for that is what Deut. 6. 5-9 implies. The

Jews tied a small fragment of the Law on their foreheads because of this command. But God asks us to have His words in our thoughts. There is perfect peace when our thoughts are "stayed" on God, Isa. 26. 3. Now how much of our "minds" has been occupied with *God's love* to-day? You may reply, and probably have already the thought in your mind, "But I cannot *make* myself love God with all my heart". True, for "the love of God is shed abroad in our hearts *by the Holy Ghost* which is given unto us", Rom. 5. 5. But even the Holy Spirit cannot do this for us without our co-operation. The Holy Spirit does only those things which bring glory to the Lord Jesus. Our Lord tells us that this is His work. "He shall glorify Me: for He shall receive of Mine and shall shew it unto you", John 16. 14. *One* way in which He does this is through the Holy Scriptures, which reveal God's love to us. We must indeed "search the Scriptures". We must KNOW God's love for us before we can love Him adequately in return. "We love Him because He first loved us", 1 John 4. 19. So we will just remind you of a few great truths concerning God's great love, its power and its preciousness.

Forty or fifty years ago an engineer, an earnest Christian man, named Clough, retired when well over middle age. He felt God calling him to the mission field. No missionary society was willing to send him out. He offered to go at his own charges; but was told he would never be able to learn the language. One society, however, suggested that he could go out to Tinnivelly and live in a mission house for a few months, and then return home to stir up missionary interest. He gladly accepted the offer. On the voyage out he learnt from a returning missionary to repeat John 3. 16 in the language of the people. On arrival he quickly picked up from a native Christian the *exact* pronunciation of the words.

With great joy he told to all whom he met, that glorious message: "God so loved the world, that He gave His only begotten Son, that whosoever believeth in Him should not perish, but have everlasting life". His happy, radiant face served to make this good news all the greater. Now the missionaries and native Christians were all bemoaning the fact that a famine was imminent because of the prolonged drought.

Clough, on the other hand, with the eye of a civil engineer, saw how it could be averted once and for all. He devised a system of irrigation, and proved to the English administrators that it was possible to carry out his plan. They promised to finance the scheme. Thousands of natives were set to work. They rejoiced at the wage! Day after day he repeated his message from the Bible. His whole sermon was simply: "God so loved the world, that whosoever believeth in Him should not perish, but have everlasting life". Those simple heathen folk gladly believed the amazing news of a God Who *loved*. In twelve months time the missionaries baptised more than 1100 converts, won for the Saviour by the knowledge of His love.

> "Wonderful things in the Bible I see,
> This is the greatest, that Jesus loves *Me*."

But Why Should *I* Suffer?

There was never so much suffering and sorrow on this earth before as there is to-day. My firm belief is that these are the days our Lord foretold when He said: "For then shall be great tribulation, such as was not since the beginning of the world to this time, no, nor ever shall be. And except those days should be shortened, there should no flesh be saved; but for the elect's sake those days shall be shortened", Matt. 24. 21, 22.

But we are all inclined to be self-centred; and we are apt to say, or at least to think: "Why should *I* suffer?"

We cannot discuss this question, and only raise the point because pain and suffering seem to be just the reverse of joy unspeakable and full of GLORY. Now let us remember that "None of us liveth to Himself", Rom. 14. 7. We reminded you that God allowed suffering and loss to come to Job in order to *prove* to Satan and his "angels" that Job would still remain true to God, even if he lost all. And Job did not fail God. You and I may not be a lesson-book to Satan—I do not know. But we are eagerly watched by the angelic host. Moreover, Satan's followers on earth have sharp eyes and are only too glad to scoff at our "religion" and our Saviour. "The wicked watcheth the righteous", Psa. 37. 32. You can guess their thoughts and their exultation if they hear us grumble and complain when pain, or illness, or tribulation befall us. But if we, like the persecuted Apostle Paul, are always rejoicing even in our tribulation, the "wicked" are greatly impressed, and are often won for Christ as a result. (See the story of the godless Major in India who became a radiant Christian because of the joy remaining in a missionary who had lost his only child, page 83.)

Would you not be willing to suffer a little, if that suffering meant the salvation of another? Just a little grumbling "switches off" our JOY unspeakable. "It is God which worketh in you both to will and to do of His good pleasure", Phil. 2. 13; and shall *His* good pleasure be *your* displeasure? Surely not! So "do all things without murmurings and disputings: that ye may be blameless and *harmless*, the sons of God without rebuke in the midst of a crooked and perverse nation, among whom ye SHINE as lights in the world", Phil. 2. 14, 15. *Try it for one day*. Not a murmur, or grumble, or complaining, or criticism at home or outside. Keep your mind stayed on the Lord Jesus: for *He* also "watches the righteous", and watches over them, and dwells *in* them.

God loves these godless folk, who are often so bright

and cheerful—full of fun and of kindly deeds; and He
wants to *win* them through you and through me. So the
Saviour sometimes asks us "to fill up that which is behind
of the afflictions of Christ . . . for His body's sake, which
is the Church" (*i.e.* all believers). He wants to reveal, "to
make known what is the riches of the GLORY . . . among
the Gentiles; which is Christ IN you, the hope of glory",
Col. 1. 24, 27.

But Christ also wants to use us as a blessing to other
Christians. Never criticize them: show them a better
way. Are we not apt to behave our *worst* in our own
homes, where we are treated best? We have a duty
there, for our bodily sufferings often keep us "prisoners"
indoors. May we let the joy and glory be the greater
when our sufferings are greatest.

What a veritable benediction a single *utterance* may
be! Ten years ago a Christian boy of 14 or 15 years old
had a nasty bicycle accident. I met him wheeling his
bicycle. His leg was cut open, and a front tooth broken.
When I said how *sorry* I was that he had crashed so badly,
he smilingly answered: "Oh, it's quite all right! It's
one of the ALL things", Rom. 8. 28. A simple word, yet
one which will never be forgotten by me. Scores of times
it has been on my own lips; and literally *hundreds* of
times it has flashed through my mind when my plans
have been upset, or things have gone wrong. Let us ever
remember that disappointments are HIS appointments.

The first recorded words that were ever spoken to our
Lord were these: "Son, why hast Thou dealt with us
thus?" And, singularly enough, that is a complaint
which has been on the lips and in the thoughts of everyone ever since. "Why has Christ, the Son of God, dealt
with me thus?" WHY? "For our light affliction, which
is but for a moment, worketh for us a far more exceeding
and eternal weight of GLORY", 2 Cor. 4. 17.

CHAPTER X

God's Best

"GOD'S best." Do not these words *hurt* us: even shock us? God has no "second best" to give us, or anyone. "Good is all that He can bless", as the hymn truly declares. Yet we verily think that most Christians —in fact *all* of us at times—believe that God is not doing His best for us. This must grieve the loving heart of the Saviour. Can we find the remedy for such want of trust and lack of faith? Yes, we surely can do so.

The Holy Spirit inspired Paul to say two of the most comforting things that lovers of the Lord Jesus could possibly know. Let us think quietly over them. And let us examine ourselves, our hearts and our lives, and find out if we *really believe* them. One of them is found in Philippians 4. 19: "But my God shall supply all your need, according to His riches in GLORY, by Christ Jesus". Surely we can ask for nothing greater than this? Now do not alter those words even in your thoughts. Let them stand as they are!

A dear friend who has passed within the veil, said that he was once a guest of a very wealthy American. In that home of luxury he saw a motto card hanging on the wall. It read, "My God shall supply all your need *out of* His riches in Glory by Christ Jesus". He quietly remarked, "I should not like to hang up *that* motto in my room". The American at once replied, "Wa'll, *I* think its just *great*". "Yes, indeed", came the retort: "It *is* great, but it might be greater. My Bible reads, 'My God shall supply all your need *according* to His riches in glory by Christ Jesus'." "So!" came the answer, "but that amounts to the same thing!" "My friend", said Dr. Marsh, "if *you* gave a beggar ten cents, it would be *out of* your riches; but if you gave him *according to* your riches he would never need to beg again". What a glorious light that remark throws on that text.

The Bible command still holds, "Be careful for nothing" —*i.e.* do not be anxious, distracted—don't worry. (Our Lord used the same word when gently reproving Martha, Luke 10. 41. But Phil. 4. 6 goes on to say, "Be careful for nothing, but in everything by prayer and supplication with thanksgiving let your requests be made known unto God". The word "supplication" means "ply upon ply" —we might add, "for supply upon supply".

> "For His love and power are such,
> None can ever ask too much."

We must not be anxious, but we must always remain "beggars" at the throne of grace. God desires us to put our requests into words, so that we *think out* what we really want. He desires us to pray, because He loves our prayer-fellowship.

Then have you ever asked yourself what those words "riches in GLORY" mean? They surely cannot imply that God stores "riches" in heaven? Our Lord's glory is in Himself, the revelation of Himself in all His words and deeds. Because these show mankind what God the Father is like. Riches so great that He could say, "He that hath seen Me hath seen the Father". He assures us that the Heavenly Father Who feeds the birds of the air, will most surely feed us; and that if God clothes the grass of the fields, and the lilies, "shall He not much more clothe" us? "But seek ye first the Kingdom of God and His righteousness", is what He bids us do, Matt. 6. 25-33. *Those* are Christ's riches in GLORY. Those are the things St. John was thinking of when he said, "The Word was

made flesh and dwelt among us, and we beheld His glory
(the glory as of the only begotten of the Father), full
of grace and truth", John 1. 14.

God undertakes to supply all our spiritual, as well as
our physical, needs.

The other verse, which is a marvellous revelation of
God's great love, is given us in Rom. 8. 28. We all know
it by heart, but have we *"taken it to heart"*? Remember
that it was written by one who underwent unparalleled
suffering, persecution, and ill-treatment extending over
many years. What is he inspired to say? "We know
that all things work together for good to them that love
God."

If you and I really believe this, and act and speak in
a way that shows we believe it, "our lives would be all
sunshine in the glory of the Lord". So we venture to
put out this challenge to every reader: Are you willing
fully to trust the Holy Spirit? Are you willing, whatever
may befall you, to say gladly, joyfully, and whole-
heartedly, "I believe God, and desire by life and lip to
live as one who KNOWS that all that befalls me is for my
highest good"? But remember that a mere *resolution*
is not enough. Moreover, there is a very definite condition added. These things are "for THEM THAT LOVE
GOD". We sometimes sing:

> "Lord, it is my chief complaint,
> That my love is cold and faint;
> But I love Thee and adore!
> O, for grace to love Thee more!"

This is a very *common* complaint. But the same Lord
Jesus Who said, "This is the first and great *commandment*,
Thou shalt LOVE the Lord Thy God with all thy heart,
and with all thy soul, and with all thy MIND", Matt.
22. 37, 38, is He Who dwells within our hearts to enable
us to do this.

The very purpose of this book is to endeavour to remind every reader how greatly the Lord Jesus loves us: for *that* knowledge alone will enable us to love Him as we ought.

The Holy Spirit *could* not have inspired Paul to write Rom. 8. 28 unless the apostle practised what he preached. Nor could He have inspired him to write to the Philippian Christians in the way he did, if "all his need" had not been "supplied" by God. Paul, who suffered unparalleled persecution and suffering, knew what it was to love Christ Jesus "with joy unspeakable and full of glory". It was this joy which made Paul and Silas sing aloud in that Philippian prison—down there in the innermost dungeon in the darkness of night. Think of it! Singing away at midnight, their backs raw and bleeding, and with their feet fast in the stocks, "Paul and Silas prayed, and sang praises unto God, and the prisoners heard them", Acts 16. 25. Such a thing could never have happened before.

"All things work together for good to them that love God." Do you suppose Paul believed this, when that poor demon-possessed girl followed himself and Silas about the city "many days" crying, day after day, "These men are the servants of the Most high God which shew unto us the way of salvation"? Acts 16. 17. I am quite *sure* he did; for had he not done so he would have cast out the evil spirit on the very first day. But we are equally sure that he did not foresee what a blessing this "annoyance" would bring.

No doubt the girl's "masters" were pleased at the advertisement given to themselves, and at the greater gain which would be theirs, ver. 19. But *after many days* "Paul . . . turned and said to the spirit, I command thee in the name of Jesus Christ to come out of her", ver. 18. And he came out. The magistrates heard all about this deed;

and no doubt the governor of the prisoner—the jailer—was also told all about it, and that was the reason why the magistrates charged him to keep Paul and Silas safely. He must have retired to rest that night wondering what that spirit-possessed girl meant when she cried over and over again: "These men are servants of the Most High God which shew unto us the way of salvation". So, when at midnight a great earthquake shook the foundations of the prison and awakened the governor, he was greatly relieved to find that all the prisoners were safe; so "He sprang in, and came trembling, and fell down before Paul and Silas . . . and said, Sirs, *what must I do to be saved*?" 29, 30. Yes, indeed, that persistent cry of the demon-possessed girl led to the conversion of that jailer, and he "rejoiced, believing in God with all his house", Acts 16. 34. God has a purpose in all He allows to befall.

"What shall we say then to these things? If God be for us, who can be against us? He that spared not His own Son, but delivered Him up for us all, how shall He not with Him also freely give us ALL THINGS"—the "all things" that work together for our good, Rom. 8. 31, 32.

Before we leave this most important and most comforting subject, let us just ask ourselves one question: Can you think of any possible reason why God should not do His best for us? It is absolutely certain that you cannot.

No one who believes on the Lord Jesus Christ can doubt His love, or His power or His presence dwelling in our hearts by faith. Even the Psalmist in his day was certain of this, that "They that seek the Lord shall not want any good thing", Psa. 34. 10.

> "He knows, He loves, He cares,
>   Nothing this truth shall dim;
> He does the very best for those
>   Who leave the choice to Him."

Now this is a matter of such great importance that it is necessary to be very explicit.

We *know* that our loving Heavenly Father chose us in Christ Jesus, "before the foundation of the world, that we should be HOLY and without BLAME before Him in LOVE".

That we should be "to the praise of the glory of His grace". This is not only His will, but also "according to the good pleasure of His will". God has very definitely promised (1) To supply ALL our need; (2) And that ALL things that happen to us, or befall us are working together for our good, Eph. 1. 4-6.

It is therefore quite obvious that any anxiety, or worry, or impatience, or annoyance, or irritation are very definitely *sinful*.

> If we worry, we do not trust;
> If we trust we do not worry.

"Worry" spells DARKNESS; "trust" spells LIGHT. Please do not give the usual answer, "I can't help worrying—worrying over my boy in the forces; worrying over my health; worrying over everything!" No, *you* cannot help worrying; but God can take away *all* worry, and every care. But He does it, not only *because* He loves us, but BY His love. That is the secret.

"Holy . . . without blame, before Him IN LOVE", Eph. 1. 4. We must *know* the love of God so fully that we love Him in return. "Perfect love casteth out fear" and worry, 1 John 4. 18. Fear of man, fear of the future, fear of the past. "The Lord God will go *before* you; and the God of Israel will be your rereward", Isa. 52. 12. He as our re-reward will guard us from fear of the sins of the past overtaking us.

Our Saviour is the only "perfect love". He dwells in our hearts by faith, Eph. 3. 17; and HE IS ALWAYS ENOUGH.

How often we unintentionally injure the faith of other people by expressing our "deep sympathy" with them in their trouble, or sorrow, or bereavement, or pain! Do not be surprised at such a strange remark. Have we not often tried to awaken sympathy for ourselves when in pain or suffering? But are we not undermining a belief in God's goodness? We are hinting that God is not *doing His best* for us! What a slander upon our loving Saviour. Let us beware *how* we express our sympathy. Everything that happens to us is allowed of God, and is for "the furtherance of the Gospel". St. Paul wrote that to his Philippian converts, Phil. 1. 12. What a deep impression that trustful triumphant note must have made on the governor of the prison and upon all who saw Paul so cruelly beaten.

When we are overtaken by any of the so-called "ills" of life, let us rejoice in being able to show our complete confidence in our loving Heavenly Father.

It is when the LIGHT *shines out of darkness* that it causes the greatest wonder and joy. That is what the Lord Jesus wants to do for us. *He* dwells in our hearts by faith in order to SHINE there, and reveal Himself there. And the darker our path, the more wonderful the light appears to be.

St. Paul writes: "For God, Who commanded the light to shine out of darkness, hath shined IN our hearts to GIVE the light of the knowledge of the glory of God in the face of Jesus Christ", 2 Cor. 4. 6. There is no excellency in *us*, no power in *us*; it is all in Christ Who dwells in us. And He desires to *shine* there, IN our hearts. So Paul regards trouble, distress, perplexity, persecution, "cast-downness", *all of them*, as opportunities for revealing the power of the Lord Jesus to use them for showing forth in us, and through us, HIMSELF: "the life also of JESUS made manifest IN our body", 2 Cor. 4. 7-11. "Whenever the Holy Spirit sees a chance

6

of glorifying Christ, He will take your whole personality and simply make it glow and blaze with a personal, passionate devotion to the Lord Jesus."

A friend of mine told me that she had recently visited a poor old lady who had suffered much pain and disappointment. "I *am* sorry," exclaimed the visitor; "so sorry for you. Providence has indeed been very hard on you."

"Yes, he has, mum," she replied, "But there's One above Who won't let him have *all* his own way!"

After a long and tiring journey from Boulogne to Marseilles, it was a relief to board the P. & O. steamer which was to take me to India. Making my way to my cabin, I drew out my steel trunk which had journeyed from Tilbury. It was, of course, securely locked; and to my great surprise and discomfiture, I found I had lost the key. What was to be done? The cabin door was opened and my cabin companion entered. With an exclamation of surprise he cried: "Why sir, I heard you preach in our school chapel last term". After a handshake he was quickly told of my lost key. "Here's my bunch," said he, "try them". With great relief I found the very key I needed. "You may keep it," said he, "I've lost the trunk". It was just "one of the all things," but I wonder—did I show any annoyance, or worry? Was it an opportunity lost?

But lunch-time had arrived. A fine soldierly-looking man came to occupy the chair on my right. I noticed that he stood behind his seat for a moment with bowed head. *Grace.*

Almost my first remark was, "How delightful to be on the way to India". "Yes," was his reply; "for *you*, perhaps, but not for me. I've left my two boys at school in England." He mentioned the two schools, so I asked him his name. "Singularly enough," as we so carelessly say, both of his boys were known to me, and only a few days before one of them had written me saying he hoped I should meet his father in India! Just one of the "all things". But my reason for telling this incident is just this. It has long been my habit to find out how people came to know Christ as a personal Saviour. The good Major was soon asked to relate his story. May I give it in his own words?

THE MAJOR'S STORY

When I went to India, I made up my mind I would have a good time—and I *did*. After a time I married a girl after my own heart and we went the pace. Worldliness, and wickedness, and wine. Then a sudden blow came. My wife fell ill and died; and I cursed God to His face! Why had He robbed me of my wife? Why this great sorrow? What harm had I done anyone? I became like a bear with a sore head. A few weeks afterwards my syce said: "Sahib, have you heard the news? The missionary Sahib's little baby, the only child, is dead!" Well—what did that matter to me? I had no interest in missionaries. Yes, I knew that this special missionary had left a home of luxury to come out and preach the Gospel; but I regarded all missionaries as fanatics—one religion was as good, or as bad, as another. Moreover, I was quite convinced that the missionary Sahib would also be cursing God for robbing him of his child; and something led me to call and see him. Perhaps I sought a little sympathy for myself.

Recalling the syce, I bade him bring my horse along, and I rode off to the mission-house. What a bright and happy welcome they gave me. The missionary Sahib was all smiles. He and his good wife were confident that all was well: that God knew best and was working His purposes out.

After a cup of tea, I asked him if he could spare time for a little talk, and we adjourned to his study. He was radiantly happy. At last I broke down and begged him to show me how I could get Christ as my Saviour. And now my one desire is to win my men for Christ.

Comment is really unnecessary; but we see how God could *trust* that missionary, by calling upon him to part with his child, and rely upon him to reveal complete confidence in God's love and goodness even in bereavement.

God's love never fails. God never makes a mistake. "We KNOW that all things work together for good to them that love God." May God enable us always to *show* that we know this; and that in sorrow or in joy we may always "be to the praise of the glory of His grace".

* * * * * *

PRAYER. O God, by the marvellous Atonement of Jesus Christ, applied to me by the Blessed Holy Spirit, cleanse the thoughts of my heart, and purify the springs of my *unconscious* life until the temper of my mind is unblameable in Thy sight. Put a right spirit within me, and whatever befalls me may I always go on my way rejoicing that I know that ALL THINGS work together for good to them that love Thee.

* * * * * *

"His divine power hath given unto us all things that pertain unto life and GODLINESS, through the knowledge of Him that hath called us to GLORY and virtue: whereby are given unto us exceeding great and precious promises, that by these ye might be partakers of the divine nature", 2 Pet. 1. 3, 4.

CHAPTER XI

As a Man Thinketh

THE highest bliss, the greatest joy, which it is possible for us to possess is to have God pouring His wondrous love into our hearts, and to have our love rising in full tide in gratitude to Him, and through our hearts to the blessing of others. To experience this is, for anyone, "heaven on earth"; for is not this the very joy of heaven?

Why is it that even very wicked men hope to be able to "make peace with God" at the end of their lives, so as to go to heaven? Why do they wish to get there? What will they *do* there, or enjoy there?

Now God's greatest desire for you and for me is that we should be so full of the glory of God, and so full of "the joy of the Lord", that the careless, and thoughtless, and godless people around us should be attracted to Him, and should see the *beauty* of holiness in us. Did you ever think of that? If the godless around us are to see such "beauty" it will only be as we mix among them in our ordinary everyday life. How much of God's *beauty* have we revealed to others to-day?

We are bidden to "worship the Lord in the beauty of holiness", but to do this we must possess this holiness and let it be seen in our everyday walk and life. Only thus can we "give unto the Lord the glory due unto His name", 1 Chron. 16. 29. King David said: *"One thing have I desired of the Lord, that will I seek after . . . to behold the beauty of the Lord"*, Psa. 27. 4. And Moses prayed: "Let the beauty of the Lord our God be upon us", Psa. 90. 17 (a prayer of Moses the man of God). "Worship the Lord in the beauty of holiness".

Please do not regard all this as fanciful. When King Jehoshaphat was in great distress because of threatened invasion, he went out to his army and stood and cried: "Believe in the Lord your God!" Then he appointed singers unto the Lord, that they should "praise the BEAUTY OF HOLINESS as they went out before the army, and to say, Praise the Lord", 2 Chron. 20. 20, 21. Now if they could do this before a battle, *we* can do this by our lives and conversation as we live our daily life.

One can anticipate your question. It is this: But how is this possible? How can it be done? The best illustration I can think of is that of Brother Lawrence, who lived 250 years ago. He wrote no book, preached no sermons, took up no "active Christian work" (as we say) for the Master. All we know about him is from a few letters he wrote! No book has so moved me to the very depth, and thrilled me with greater blessing than the little collection of the letters he wrote. Its title is "The Practice of the Presence of God". He was no great scholar. He was no clever workman. He lost his jobs as a footman because of his clumsiness.

In despair, he sought the refuge of a monastery, and there they put him in the kitchen, to do menial duties to which he had naturally a great aversion; and there he worked for forty years. And there he died on Feb. 6, 1691. What chance has a man to devote his life to the service of God in such a menial position; not even able "to take up a little bit of work for God", as we sometimes ask *our* people to do?

How came this clumsy workman to live such a beautiful life that reports of it spread far and wide? Bishops and other great men went to the monastery to see him and ask him the secret of it!

The "secret" is such a simple one that anyone can put it into practice.

For the first ten years in the kitchen he suffered much.

He says: "My *mind* was centred on *myself*, always fearing that I was not as devoted to God as I wished to be, and thinking of my past sins. Then I found myself changed all at once, and my soul, which up till that time was in trouble, felt a profound inward peace, as if it had found its centre and place of rest. Ever since then I have been, and now am, walking before God in simple faith with humility and love; and I apply myself diligently to *do* nothing, say nothing, and *think* nothing which *may* displease Him. May He do with me what He pleases. I have no will but the will of God. I make it my only business to persevere in His holy presence, wherein *I keep myself* by a simple attention, and an absorbing passionate regard to God; an actual presence of God—a silent and secret constant intercourse of the soul with God, which often causes me joy and raptures inwardly—and sometimes also outwardly—so great that I am forced to use means to moderate them". "I desire only Him."

Remember that it is not a religious recluse who speaks like this. His life was a very busy and exacting one. Yet he declares: "I am more united to God in my ordinary occupations, than when I leave them for my devotions in retirement".

He feared nothing, and had no occasion to take counsel with anyone about his soul. He did everything purely for the love of God. Prayer, to him, was nothing else than a sense of God's presence, his soul being at that time insensible to everything but Divine LOVE. When prayer-time passed, he still continued with God, praising and blessing Him with all his might, so that he passed his life in continual JOY. He did little things for the love of God; "for," said he, "God looks not at the greatness of the work, but at the *love with which it is performed*".

He said that he came to this condition—this state of heart and mind—by regarding God as the end of all his thoughts and desires. He endeavoured to live in a continual sense of His presence, and never to forget Him more. "In the noise and clatter of the kitchen", said he, "I possess God in as great tranquillity as if I were on my knees at the blessed sacrament".

A week before he died he wrote: "If we knew how much He loves us, we should be always ready to receive equally and with indifference the sweet and the bitter from His hands; all would please that came from Him. Let all our business be to know God. The deeper our knowledge the greater will be our love. He is within us: seek Him not elsewhere. He would possess our hearts alone."

What Brother Lawrence did, you and I can do. Nay, more, *we* have a greater incentive than *he* had. He does not seem to have been allowed to possess or *read* a Bible. There is not a single reference to Scripture in his writings.

But *we* have the knowledge of God's clear commands and promises. Are we not bidden to bring "into captivity *every* THOUGHT to the obedience of Christ"? 2 Cor. 10. 5. Scripture says, "Whether therefore ye eat, or drink, or whatsoever ye do, do all to the glory of God", 1 Cor. 10. 31.

Then there is the Divine command:

"Whatsoever ye do, do it heartily as to the Lord, and not unto men. Whatsoever ye do in word or deed, do all in the Name of the Lord Jesus", Col. 3. 23, 17. We cannot obey such commands without keeping God constantly in our *thoughts*. "Let the word of Christ dwell in you richly in all wisdom, ver. 16; this must mean in our thoughts, and infers that we have a *knowledge* of the Word of Christ.

Then we read, "Be careful for (anxious about) nothing, but in *every thing* by prayer and supplication with thanksgiving let your requests be made known unto God". And as a result of such an attitude towards our Heavenly Father, we read: "And the peace of God, which passeth all under-

standing shall keep your hearts and MINDS through Christ
Jesus". Then comes the comprehensive exhortation:
"Finally, whatsoever things are true, whatsoever things
are honest . . . just . . . pure . . . lovely . . . of good report;
if there be any virtue, . . . any praise, THINK ON THESE
THINGS". Phil. 4. 6-8.

"Rejoice in the Lord *alway*: and again I say, RE-
JOICE", ver. 4. Do you not see that all these things are
impossible to us unless our *thoughts* are fixed on God and
His love? Are we not given the promise: "Thou wilt
keep him in perfect peace, whose *mind* is stayed on
Thee". Why? "Because he trusteth in Thee", Isa. 26. 3.

Meditate on these few words—a "mind stayed on
God". The word "stayed" (in Hebrew) means "supported"
or "sustained". The "mind" of Brother Lawrence
simply rested constantly on God. He said: "I am
assured beyond all doubt that my soul has been with
God these past thirty years and more. He converses
with me and delights Himself with me unceasingly in a
thousand ways. I beseech Him to render me entirely
like Himself, and to fashion in my soul His perfect image.
May He do with me what He pleases. I desire only Him,
and would fain be wholly devoted to Him."

Again and again in the few letters he wrote to his
friends, he lays the greatest stress on this: "Let us think
of Him unceasingly: in Him let us put our whole confidence. How can we pray to Him but in *thinking* of Him
often? And how can we have Him often in our thoughts
except by a holy *habit* of thought which we should
form? We must KNOW before we can love. And to know
we must *think of* Him. Often think on God by day and
by night; in your business and in your pleasures. He is
always near you, and with you, and IN you. Leave Him
not alone. Adore him unceasingly. This is the glorious
employment of a Christian. Acquire the habit of holding

constant converse with God, and forget Him the least you can." "Peace of soul and repose of spirit descend on me in sleep. I am in a calm so great that I fear nothing. What can I fear when I am with Him—or rather He with me?" "We have a God Who is infinitely gracious, and knows all our wants. A little lifting up of the heart to Him suffices; a little remembrance of God; one act of inward worship. Think of God the most you can. Hold yourself in prayer before God. Let it be your business to keep your mind in the presence of God. Think of Him often. Let us think often that our only business in this life is to please God—loving and serving God. Let us think of Him unceasingly; and in Him let us put our whole confidence."

That was the only message Brother Lawrence had. Probably no man living in his days exercised such a powerful and widespread influence for good. And how Scriptural it all is! God honours His Word. May we therefore call your attention to what the Holy Scriptures tell us?

"We have the mind of Christ", 1 Cor. 2. 16.

"Pray without ceasing", 1 Thess. 5. 17.

"I was daily his delight, rejoicing always before Him. . . . My delights were with the sons of men", Prov. 8. 30-31.

"Lo I am with you alway, even unto the end of the world", Matt. 28. 20.

"That Christ may dwell in your hearts by faith", Eph. 3. 17.

"The mystery . . . hid from ages . . . but now is made manifest to His saints: to whom God would make known what is the RICHES OF THE GLORY of this mystery among the Gentiles (*i.e. you* and *me*): which is CHRIST *in* YOU the hope of glory", Col. 1. 26, 27.

"He giveth His beloved sleep", Psa. 127. 2, Amer. V., R.V.

"As a man thinketh in his heart so is he", Prov. 23. 7.

"I love them that love Me; and they that seek me early shall find Me", Prov. 8. 17.

My thoughts are not your thoughts. If ever a man lived whose mind was "stayed on God" it was Brother Lawrence. That great aim—perhaps the greatest of all aims—was not merely the theme of the few letters he wrote, and the conversations that are related to us—it was the one great aim of his life, and has been an incentive to tens of thousands of others to "go and do likewise". You may say, "Yes, but he had as his companions and fellow-workers, none but men whose whole lives were supposed to be wholly devoted to God". That is true, but such people are often *the most difficult to get on with.* We so often quarrel with one another, because we do not see "eye to eye" on some matter of doctrine or ritual.

An earnest evangelical Vicar lived opposite an advanced Anglo-Catholic Vicar. They were not on speaking terms with each other; yet both were children of the same Heavenly Father, and both zealous workers for the Master. The climax came. Let me repeat what the Evangelical Vicar told me himself: "One day I met the Anglo-Catholic man. I stopped him and said to him, 'You are a *traitor* to your Church. You ought to be thoroughly ashamed of yourself.' Then I walked angrily away. When I returned home I told my wife what had happened. Her kindly, quietly-spoken reply was: 'And what *good* do you think it has done?' 'Good! Well, he knows what some of us *think* of him.' 'And will *that* do any good?' I began to wonder! As I lay awake that night I came to realise how unchristian I had been. The next morning, after a hasty breakfast, I hurried across to the Vicarage opposite, and confessed to my 'enemy' how wicked I felt at my rudeness to him. He displayed such a kindly, forgiving, loving spirit that my heart warmed toward him. And now we are bosom friends, although neither of us has altered his religious views one little bit".

What had happened? My friend had merely changed his thought-life concerning a fellow-Christian. Are you wondering why that incident is suddenly dragged in? *Cease* to wonder. Do you not see that the good Vicar's *thought-life* was completely changed by a kindly remonstrance from his wife?—truly his "better half".

You and I are constantly influencing the thought-life of all whom we meet. We do it by the look on our faces, or the courtesy of our manner, or the patient way in which we wait our turn to be served in shops, or the kindly way we stand aside when a later arrival pushes forward out of her turn.

Do we *always* show a forbearing spirit in our home-life? Are we always truly helpful and loving and considerate there? A lady consulted a friend of mine about her difficulties with her husband. He was *impossible*, and she could no longer live with him. Her good pastor let her tell him all about it. Then he replied: "It is evident that you are far more careful about the polish on your lino- leum than about the smile on your face. Go home and think about it." The impossible husband became more than possible.

You mothers! Think of your great influence in the home. Your children will never forget it, for good or for ill.

In one Midland parish the Vicar's wife takes a Sunday class of lads of ten or eleven years old. She told me this beautiful incident. Her lesson one Sunday afternoon was about the Prodigal Son. The boys listened spell- bound. Then one of them said: "Please, Miss — what did his muvver think about it?" Before she could answer, another laddie burst out with: "Please, Miss, I don't think his muvver could have been alive! It wouldn't have happened if his *muvver* had been alive!" We can visualise the kind of mother *that* little boy had. Just think of a mother's influence! Think of the power we exert over the thoughts and lives of the various people we meet. Do we *realise* it? The Lord Jesus said:

"I am the Light of the world", John 8. 12.

"Ye are the light of the world", Matt. 5. 14.

But our Saviour also said: "If therefore the LIGHT that is in thee be *darkness*, how great is that darkness", Matt. 6. 23. What can He mean? How is it possible for "light" to be "darkness"? It is, to all intents and purposes, DARKNESS when we refuse to let it shine out to others.

Do you remember how Zacharias became *dumb* because of his unbelief? When "his tongue loosed, and he spake and praised God", Luke 1. 64, he said of his son John: "And thou, child, shalt be called the prophet of the Highest . . . to *give knowledge* of salvation unto His people . . . to give LIGHT to them that sit in *darkness*", verses 76-79. That is also *our* duty, our amazing privilege.

Are we giving "light" to anyone? Every believer on the Lord Jesus can rejoice in the glorious thought: "I am come a light into the world", John 12. 46. Not our *own* light, or reflected light, but because THE Light of the world dwells in us, and we reveal Him to all around.

We are "children of light", John 12. 36. "Now are ye light in the Lord: WALK AS CHILDREN OF LIGHT", Eph. 5. 8. "Ye are ALL the children of light", 1 Thess. 5. 5. If you light a candle it is for the purpose of using its light. We do not light a candle to put it in a *secret place*, or under a measure (a "bushel", representing our business, our occupation) or under a bed where it cannot be seen (slothfulness): "but on a candlestick that they which come in may see the LIGHT", Luke 11. 33. "The spirit of man is the candle of the Lord", Prov. 20. 27.

Secret Christians are of no use to God or man; and they may be worse than useless. "Look at these religious folk, buttonholing you about religion," said a godless man to a friend. "You make no profession about religion, yet you live a straight and clean life! I shall be quite content to be like you." The listener became very grave. Then he replied: "God forgive me. I *am* a religious man; and I owe all to Jesus Christ, but I have been a *secret* Christian."

Believe me, the happiest and the most joyous life is that of a child of God whose aim in life is to reveal something of the beauty of the Lord in every look, and word and deed—a man who is just a "light" in the world. A light is something which shines without any fuss, or noise, or effort, because that would attract attention to *itself*. A spluttering candle or singing gas jet or winking electric light causes us to ask: What's the matter with the *light*. A light shines not to reveal itself, but to reveal objects outside of it. In fact, light *itself* is not visible. Its existence is known only by what it reveals. *We* are to be lights to reveal the beauty of the Lord. "Let the beauty of the Lord our God be upon us", Psa. 90. 17. The Lord Jesus depends upon us. *Ours* are the only eyes He looks out of upon the world. Ours are the only feet to run His errands, ours are the only lips He has to speak through. Shall we keep them only for our own purposes?

Arthur Burroughs, the late Bishop of Ripon, said: "The measure of what you can do for the world will be simply *what you let God do* with yourself. With most of us God can do so little because we are so little between His hands. For how long, I wonder, in an ordinary day? Is it as much as half-an-hour in the twenty-four? And then we are surprised that so little happens! No, if we are to be God's men and to wield God's power, we must arrange to give Him more access *to* us, and He Himself will find His own passage *through* us."

The reason for our past failures is that we never *thought* of these things. Dare we, shall we, resolve that henceforth we will bear in mind, as a joyous exhilarating thought, that we are God's children—children of the light; and that in all our actions, words, and behaviour we may be SHINING "as lights in the world, holding forth the word of life", Phil. 2. 15, 16.

Chapter XII

Sons of God

HAVE we, in these days of marvel, lost the secret of wonder? Have you never in your life said to yourself: "How I wish I could approach the Holy Scriptures as one who had never read the Bible before? What a thrill one would feel! It's statements would appear to be absolutely incredible to us. Even the simple fact that God—an almighty, omniscient, exalted God—should take any real interest in us as individuals, would seem almost absurd; and that He should take any pains to direct our lives, and even to plan them for us, would astonish us greatly. But what would be our amazement to find that He LOVES us, and adopts us into His family and calls us children of God?"

But is it not a far greater "marvel" that most Church-goers have never given five consecutive minutes just to think over what it means, and entails, and involves to be LOVED BY GOD?

When Jesus of Nazareth left His home, and His work as a carpenter, and went to Jordan to be baptized by John the Baptist, John declared that he saw the Spirit of God descending on Christ Jesus, and remaining on Him. Then he added: "And I saw and bare record that this is the Son of God". Then on two consecutive days he cried to the crowd of listeners: "BEHOLD the Lamb of God!" That cry led John and Andrew to follow Jesus, John 1. 29-37.

But to us who are His followers, however "afar off" we follow, there is a very precious word. John himself gives it in his first epistle: "BEHOLD what manner of love the

Father hath bestowed on us, that we should be called the sons of God, and *we are*", 1 John 3. 1, R.V.

Then the "beloved disciple" goes on to say: "Beloved, now are we the sons of God, and it doth not yet appear what we shall be: but we know that when He shall appear, we shall be like Him; for we shall see Him as He is", verse 2.

But God calls us to be like the Lord Jesus now, to-day, in this brief life of ours when we *see* Him, if only by faith. "But now we see not yet all things put under Him. But we SEE JESUS . . . crowned with glory and honour", Heb. 2. 8-9. And that "seeing", that look, should suffice to make us "like Him". The children sing:

> "Be like Jesus! This my song,
> In the home and in the throng;
> Be like Jesus all day long—
> I would be like Jesus."

Why should not we *all* sing that chorus? Everything that happens to us is allowed by God; and if we love Him "all things *work together* for good" in order that we should be like Jesus. That is the purpose of all that our loving heavenly Father allows to happen to us. He longs for us to share the family likeness as children of God. Read Rom. 8. 28-30. Read it over and over again. Memorise it. May this utterance from God transform our lives, and enrich our witness.

"I'M A SON OF GOD."

Some years ago it was my privilege to spend some time in India. Now there was living in a fair-sized village in Tinnevelly, a man who was sorely crippled by ulcers on both legs and feet. Someone persuaded him to go to the White Doctor who lived sixty miles away. How he managed that long tramp it is difficult to imagine.

At length he arrived, and piteously pleaded to be given *"new feet"*. The medical missionary put him to bed,

7

washed and dressed those poor feet with tender care, day after day, week after week. And each day the patient listened to the Gospel message about the Divine Healer. The villager stayed on at the hospital for a few days after he was cured. The doctor would read to him from John's Gospel. One morning he read John 1— reading, of course, from a little penny Gospel in the native tongue. They reached John 1. 12, "He came unto His own, and His own received Him not. But as many as received Him, to them gave He power to become the sons of God". "Stop, Sahib," cried the healed cripple. "Stop! Is it *possible* for *any* man to become a son of God?" When the reply came, he eagerly asked, "How can *I* become a 'son of God'?" "Listen to what *God* says", replied the Missionary, with impressive, prayerful earnestness, "'even to them that believe on His Name'."

What this "believing" meant—the "receiving" Him, the Saviour of the world, *as his own personal Saviour*— was carefully explained; and, owing to previous teaching during his stay, easily understood. After a little prayer together, the native sprang up, and with a face radiant with joy, he cried, "Now *I'm a son of God*. I cannot stay. I must hurry back to my village and spread this joyful news". He begged to have a copy of the "holy book". The doctor marked St. John 1. 11, 12, and bade the new convert God-speed.

A few weeks afterwards, the patient returned with two of the leading men of the village with him. It transpired that the man who came to *know* that he was a son of God, had, on his journey home, accosted every one whom he met, with the cry: "I'm a son of God." His radiantly happy face, and the joyful ring in his voice impressed them immensely, and led to their making enquiries about this wonderful news. Several made reply: "A son of God? Well, you *look* it".

But why had he come back to the hospital? It was to

say that everyone in his village desired to become "sons of God", and that he had taught them *how* to do so from the Holy Book.

The missionary was astonished. "How could you do that?" he asked. "You cannot read!" "No," said he, "but there was a man in the village who *could* read. He read, and *I* explained it all".

Then he begged the doctor to come to the village and teach the people more, and then baptise them.

Let the obvious lesson of this story grip everyone of us. It is a joyous thing to be a son of God. May the joy beam out of our faces, and shine forth from our lives, and win others by the words of our lips. And may those lives and lips show that we firmly believe that God always does His *best* for us His children.

WHOSE CHILD IS THAT?

A workman earning good wages took to drink. He spent every evening in the public-house, and neglected his home and family. One evening, before he had "taken too much", the pub. door was pushed open, and an untidy, ill-clad, miserable little child cried, "Daddy, *do* come home; we're so hungry!" One of the men standing at the counter exclaimed angrily: "Whose child is *that*? Her father ought to be thoroughly ashamed of himself!" The father heard that scathing remark, and after a little time walked out. He *was* ashamed of himself. The wickedness of neglecting his wife and children was borne in upon him. He not only gave up the drink, but asked a Christian friend to point him to Christ as His Saviour.

Children of God, does our Heavenly Father's reputation *suffer* because of us? Are our "robes of righteousness" scanty and unworthy of our loving Saviour? If so *He* gets the blame!

Or can we truthfully and joyfully sing: "I will greatly

rejoice in the Lord, my soul shall be joyful in my God;
for He hath clothed me with the garments of salvation;
He hath covered me with the robe of righteousness . . . so
the Lord will cause righteousness and praise to spring
forth before all the nations", Isa. 61. 10-11.

> He is able,
> He is willing,
> Doubt no more.

"Thou shalt also be a crown of GLORY in the hand of the
Lord, and a royal diadem in the hand of thy God",
Isa. 62. 3. "So shall thy GOD rejoice over thee", ver. 5.

Children of God! "The Spirit itself beareth witness with
our spirit that we are children of God—and if children,
then heirs: heirs of God and joint-heirs with Christ; if
so be that we suffer with Him, that we may also be
glorified together. For I reckon that the sufferings of
this present time are not worthy to be compared with
the GLORY that shall be revealed in us", Rom. 8. 16-18.
O, let us ever bear in *mind* that Christ reveals this glory
now in this present time.

CHAPTER XIII

Though he Fall

THE greater our knowledge of the Lord Jesus and His great love for us, the more conscious we become of our own faults and failings; and the more earnest is our desire and longing to know "what is the hope of His calling, and what the riches of the glory of His inheritance in the saints", Eph. 1. 18. We yearn to be "like Jesus". None of us is perfect. Sometimes, however, a Christian worker is "overtaken in a fault", as we say. Such a thing may happen to any of us when we are not *running in the way of His commandments*", Psa. 119. 32. We usually say of such a one: "Ah, he was not himself when he did that". But what is to be our attitude toward the Christian worker who falls? Are we to avoid him; treat him coldly; cut him off from all fellowship with us? We will not answer the question now. But we would like you to think over the way the Lord Jesus treated such people. There is that great promise given to all good men in Psalm 37. 23-24: "The steps of a good man are ordered by the Lord: and He delighteth in his way. Though he fall he shall not be utterly cast down: for the Lord upholdeth him with His hand". And Christ will hold him fast. One thing is quite certain. It is, that every child of God *desires to do the right thing* toward a brother Christian who falls into grievous sin. Simon Peter "fell," and a very bad fall it was; and just when the Saviour needed him most. It was *he* who said that Christ left us an example "that we should follow His steps", 1 Pet. 2. 21. Peter alone knows what those steps were in our Lord's dealings with him. He does not tell us, but we can guess what he said to Christ and what the

Saviour said to him, when our Lord appeared to him after His resurrection, Luke 23. 34.

Christ's whole life was an example. This we cannot speak about here. We are endeavouring to learn more about God's wonderful love, so that *we, too, may show* that self-same love to all around, the love of Christ Who "dwells in our hearts by faith", Eph. 3. 17. We know the love of the Lord Jesus. Do you remember His words to religious people—Scribes and Pharisees, who openly accused another who had sinned. He pretended not to hear. But as they continued to repeat *publicly* their accusation, He quietly said, "He that is without sin among you, let him first cast a stone at her". Convicted by their own consciences, they went away one by one. "Woman," said the Saviour "hath no man condemned thee"? "No man, *Lord*." "Neither do I condemn thee: go and sin no more", John 8. 1-11.

The Saviour knew her guilt. But He knew more. He saw her true penitence. We may follow *that* example and say: "Neither will I condemn a fallen brother". He left us another example: "The Son of Man is come to seek and to save that which was lost", Luke 19. 10. On any and every occasion He sought to save sinners. His love for them was so great that He became known as "the friend of publicans and sinners". He endeavoured to win great sinners by great love. May we also seek to win back, by LOVE, any "good man" who "falls".

Do you not think that God's great love was never seen to be greater than in His dealings with Judas Iscariot? No—do not ask me *why* our Lord chose Judas as one of the twelve. A greater problem is: Why did He choose *me*? I sometimes wonder which of the twelve was the companion of Judas when Christ "sent them forth two by two: and gave them power over unclean spirits", Mark 6. 7. What a responsibility for that companion, and what an *opportunity*.

Surely the other apostles must have sometimes felt that Judas was *not quite their man*? Yet Christ's love for Judas never allowed Him to give the slightest hint that there was anything wrong with the traitor. Quite early in His ministry we are told that "Jesus knew from the beginning . . . who should betray Him," and He told the disciples this, but did not mention his name or refer to the betrayal. He gave Judas a warning when He said, "Have not I chosen you twelve, and one of you is a devil?" John 6. 64, 70. Did Judas find devils subject unto him? Mark 6. 13. Satan must have used him in this way, so that he should not appear to be different from the others.

The Lord Jesus had already given His disciples a very solemn warning. At the close of His sermon on the mount He exclaims: "Many will say to Me in that day, Lord, Lord, have we not prophesied (witnessed) in Thy Name? and in Thy Name have cast out devils? and . . . done many wonderful works? And then will I profess unto them, *I never knew you*: depart from me, ye that work iniquity", Matt. 7. 22-23.

It may be that some of us have prominent fellow-labourers who *seem to us* to be unconverted men, but who appear to be far more successful than we are in their work for the Master. What are we to do? Certainly we must not criticize them; and certainly we must pray for them, and do all in our power to be a blessing to them. How patient and how loving our Lord was with Judas. Our Saviour knows all about our difficulties, and He is counting on us. "Leaving us an example that we should follow His steps", 1 Pet. 2. 21. When a Christian worker "falls" as we say, do not "give him the cold shoulder", and shew that you despise him.

God is love, and there is probably no greater revelation of love—apart of course from the cross of Christ itself—

than that our Lord bestowed on Judas. Even to the very last He never once by word or deed revealed the man's true character. Then came that final day of our Saviour's earthly life, and He made effort after effort to bring Judas to repentance. How He loved that faulty disciple!

"Jesus, knowing that the Father had given all things into His hands, and that He was come from God, and went to God; He riseth from supper, and laid aside His garments; and took a towel, and girded Himself", John 13. 3-4. He garbed Himself as a slave, and kneeling at the feet of Judas, He washed those feet—the feet of His betrayer. It is thought that our Lord came to Judas *first of all* and to St. Peter last of all. That itself showed His love to Judas. But notice this: our Lord asked them, "Know ye what I have done to you? Ye call Me Master and Lord, and ye say well, for so I am . . . . I have given you an EXAMPLE, that ye should do as I have done to you". Then His love for Judas made Christ "troubled in spirit". He had failed to win Judas. As supper proceeded He gave Judas the "sop", an act denoting greatest *honour* to a guest. Read it over again—John 13, Christ's "example".

But this love did not stop there. The betrayer comes to Gethsemane with the chief priests and elders, and a hostile crowd with swords and staves. Judas steps forward and cries, "Hail Master, and kissed Him". The word means kissed Him heartily or thoroughly—a most friendly kiss. The Saviour showed no resentment, no recoil from the embrace of a traitor—once His "familiar friend", Psa. 41. 9—but greets him in kindly terms: "Friend" (close comrade). "Friend, wherefore art thou come?" Matt. 26. 50. What depth of love was there! Our Saviour had just *washed* that heel.

Simon Peter never forgot that scene or that love. He saw there another example to follow. You will remember how he wrote in after years: "Christ also suffered for us, leaving us an example that ye should follow His steps", 1 Pet. 2. 21.

But the purpose of this chapter is to show the amazing patience God shows with His children who fall into great sin, and His wonderful love for them. Look at Simon Peter—the only apostle who presumed to rebuke our Lord to His face. When our Lord "spake openly" about His forthcoming death on the Cross, "Peter *took Him*, and began to rebuke Him", Mark 8. 32. "This shall never be unto Thee!" Then we remember Peter's boastful reply to our Lord's words: "All ye shall be offended because of Me this night. . . ." Peter answered and said unto Him, Though all men shall be offended because of Thee, yet will I never be offended, Mark 14. 29. "Jesus said unto him, Verily, I say unto Thee, that this night, before the cock crow, Thou shalt deny Me thrice. Peter said, . . . Though I should die with Thee, yet will I not deny Thee", Matt. 26. 34, 35.

Now what a revelation of Christ's love for Peter lies in our Lord's words. After denying our Lord twice, the men warming themselves by the fire said, "Surely thou also art one of them, for thy speech bewrayeth thee." Then began he to curse and to swear, saying: "I know not the Man", Matt. 26. 69-75. "And while he yet spake, the cock crew, and the Lord turned and looked upon Peter. And Peter remembered the word of the Lord . . . and Peter went out and wept bitterly", Luke 22. 56-62. That "look" which Christ graciously gave Simon Peter was a look that conveyed infinite love and compassion. The Lord knew all about it, and the cock-crowing revealed Christ's foreknowledge and forbearance, yes, and forgiveness. Peter was weeping for gratitude as well as for penitence and sorrow.

What led to Simon Peter's grievous fall? Just his

refusal to believe our Lord's words when He foretold the Cross—His death and passion; and his want of faith in Christ's *power to defend Himself* in the garden of Gethsemane: a power which our Lord refused to use. Strange to say, it was his *love* for His Master which was his undoing. He drew his sword and struck a blow. Our Lord, in His love for His disciples, said to the servants and officers of the chief priests, "If ye seek Me, let these go their way". But Simon Peter thought our Lord needed his help. "Simon Peter, having a sword, drew it, and smote the high priest's servant, and cut off his right ear. The servant's name was Malchus", John 18. 8-10.

After Peter had twice denied our Lord, "one of the servants of the high priest, *being his kinsman whose ear Peter cut off*, saith, "Did not I see thee in the garden with Him?" Peter at once foresaw grave danger for himself. What would happen if this kinsman beckoned to Malchus, and cried out, "Come here! This is the man who cut off your ear"? It is not suprising that Peter hurried out into the darkness, weeping bitterly.

There is a very touching addition to this incident, given us by St. Mark. It is commonly believed that John Mark (who became such a close personal friend of Simon Peter that he calls him his "son", 1 Pet. 5. 13) was the certain young man who fled from Gethsemane when the Lord Jesus was seized by the soldiers, Mark 14. 51, 52.

It is also commonly believed that John Mark wrote his Gospel largely under Peter's direction; or, at all events, obtained his account of our Lord's life from Simon Peter. There is a very pathetic touch in that Gospel. Mark, in relating the story of Peter's denial of our Lord, says, "and *whenever* he thought thereon he wept bitterly" (for that is the force of the Greek), Mark 14. 72. As Peter talked to his young disciple, and recounted his inspired recollections—John 14. 26—of the

Lord's sayings and doings, Peter would sometimes burst into tears. "Master, why do you weep?" "I was thinking how I denied my Lord!"

But we are speaking about Simon Peter who "fell", and denied his Lord with oaths and curses. Have you ever meditated over the marvellous revelation of Christ's LOVE for all of us that is revealed by this incident?

We beg you to do so once more. Some Christians who will read these lines have fallen; just think over our Lord's attitude to Peter. That is how He would deal with *you*. You may have fallen, but "The eternal God is thy refuge, and underneath are the everlasting arms", Deut. 33. 27. Child of God, why are those "everlasting arms" underneath? Will God remove them when you *fall*? The great majority who take up this book will be kindly Christian people whose sins have never scandalized their friends, never brought them into disgrace. Now what will *your* attitude be to a "saint" who falls? Remember that "all have sinned, and come short of the glory of God". "There is no difference", Rom. 3. 23. Are you going to show your "righteous" indignation by at once banishing the sinner from your presence, and from your sympathy and from your friendship? God forbid! Are we to remove *our* arms of support, and drive the sinner from our "camp"? Our Saviour's love is never so clearly revealed as when He is dealing with sinners.

Think of that sinful woman dragged before the Saviour by "righteous" Scribes and Pharisees, who quoted Scripture and asked our Lord what He thought about it, John 8. 2-12. When pressed for a reply, our Lord said, "He that is without sin among you, let *him first* cast a stone at her". Those "righteous" men quietly slipped away, beginning at the eldest.

Let us think of THE *first* STONE before we speak harshly or think despisingly of a saint who falls. Then "Jesus lifted up Himself and spoke to the sinner: 'Woman, where are those thine accusers?' Hath no man condemned thee? No man, Lord. And Jesus said unto her, Neither do I condemn thee: go and sin no more."

"Then spake Jesus again . . . saying, I am the light of the world." And we are not surprised to read, "As He spake these words many believed on Him", ver. 30. But of this I am *sure*, that if the Saviour had sided with the sinners—the "righteous" Scribes and Pharisees, the exponents of the Scriptures—there would not have been a single convert that day.

Read over that hymn, "At even, ere the sun was set", and ask yourself: Where do *I* come in?

> "O Saviour Christ, our woes dispel;
> 　For some are sick, and some are sad;
> And some have never loved Thee well;
> 　And some have lost the love they had.

> "And none, O Lord, have perfect rest,
> 　For NONE are wholly free from sin;
> And they who fain would serve Thee best
> 　Are *conscious most* of wrong within."

Now let us come back to Simon Peter and his dreadful fall, because we have an earnest longing to speak words of cheer and comfort to them who "fall" to-day. How deeply the Lord Jesus *loves* us; and it is when we *fall* that He reveals His compassion and love in a very marked manner; because we *need* it so urgently. There *is* no love like the love of Jesus. I want to make you see how *hopeless* was Peter's case, *i.e.* humanly speaking.

Think of his sorrow, remorse, and absolute dejection. He *did* love the Lord. He had stood up for Him in the garden. And now *all was gone*. His Master gone—His own reputation gone. Did you ever picture his deplorable position? How could he, once the leading apostle, face his fellow-disciples again? He was for ever disgraced! We are not told a word about what they *thought* of Peter. Perhaps John, who was present at the time of the cursing and swearing and "denyings", told the others; we do not know. He *must* have overheard Peter's words. But we *do* see Peter going out into darkness and weeping bitterly. We repeat it: How could he ever face the disciples again? What happened to Peter during those three days before the resurrection we know not.

Now Peter's denial of our Lord is one of the very few incidents that are recorded in every one of the four Gospels. There must be some great reason for this, for consecrated people, if they can avoid it, never tell others of the sins and shortcomings of friends. They *pray* for them, but never blazon their faults abroad, or give their poor friends the "cold shoulder".

Just picture the man, utterly broken down, a great strong man weeping bitterly. The great apostle, now a penitent sinner. He dare not face Mary the mother of Jesus! Had John *told* her about his behaviour? Did she know? So far as we can gather, he shunned the company of the other apostles. He must also have feared recognition by the chief priest's servants if he appeared in the streets. And John "was known to the high priest". Twice we are told this in two consecutive verses, John 18. 15, 16. They might send to arrest John, and if Peter was there he would be identified as the man with a sword.

So on the morning of the resurrection he seems to have been living alone, "not worthy to be called an apostle". Not worthy to be called a disciple. And, worst of all, he had no *hope* of seeing his Blessed Master again to say how grieved he was at denying Him. What *agonies* he endured during those three days when our Lord's body lay in the tomb it is quite impossible for us to fathom. He dare not venture out—he might meet Malchus; and he would avoid the possibility of getting shunned by the other disciples of Christ. (Have *we* never "denied" our Lord?)

Now let us turn from this poor, broken, penitent, feeling utterly disgraced and disowned and helpless, to the Saviour of the world. His Spirit had ascended to the Father, Luke 23. 46. And there in Paradise with Him was the converted malefactor from the cross, vers. 39, 43. Then came our Lord's glorious resurrection from the dead, and the most amazing revelation of His LOVE for sinners; especially for the saint who falls. Brother Lawrence said: "That we ought *without anxiety*, to expect the pardon of our sins from the blood of Jesus Christ, labouring simply to love Him with all our hearts. That God seemed to have granted the greatest favours to the *greatest sinners*, as more signal monuments of His mercy". But these greatest favours are not *gained* by great sin: they result from the great love, and gratitude, and devotion, and radiant joy which flow from the heart to the Saviour Who has "forgiven much". See Luke 7. 36-47.

Picture Simon Peter, the saddest man in the world, on the morning of the resurrection. Unknown to him, the Saviour has "risen from the dead". If the story of the resurrection had been an invention, instead of a glorious certainty, it would have told of Christ Jesus appearing first of all to His sorrowing mother, and to John the disciple whom Jesus loved, and to Mary, Martha and Lazarus. But who would invent an appearance to *Simon Peter*? Are you not amazed to find that the risen Saviour's *first* appearance was, not to His beloved mother, but "to Mary Magdalene out of whom He had cast seven devils", Mark 16. 9. She was the last at the Cross and the first at the tomb.

St. Mark, the convert, and disciple, and friend of Simon Peter, tells us this most touching incident. The women saw the stone rolled away, and they peered into the tomb. There was an angel there. "And he saith unto them, Be not affrighted: ye seek Jesus of Nazareth which was crucified. He is risen, He is not here. . . . But go your way, tell His disciples *and Peter*"—AND PETER! Mark 16. 6, 7. Peter might have said, "But I am no longer worthy to be *called* a disciple". The Lord Jesus foresaw this, as He foresees all our fears and doubts, and anticipates them. "And Peter!" What a loving, gracious thoughtful touch! *"And Peter."* "The steps of a good man are ordered by the Lord; . . . though he fall he shall not be utterly cast down; for the Lord upholdeth him with His hand", Psa. 37. 23-24.

Mary Magdalene herself had fallen deeply. Tradition says she is the "woman who was a sinner" that entered Simon's house during a dinner party and washed the Saviour's feet with her tears, Luke 7. 38. She would have heard of Peter's fall. How her heart must have grieved for Him! *She* knew where to find him. We rejoice to be the bearer of good news. She, too, was filled with joy to be the first messenger to tell of His resurrection. And with a woman's intuition she ran to Peter's lodgings first, before telling the others. To *her* the message became: "Go tell PETER and His disciples".

Bishop Moule says that the Greek of John 20. 2: "She runneth and cometh *to* Simon Peter and *to* the other disciple whom Jesus loved", implies a knock at *two* doors.

It is impossible, however, to fathom the depths of the love of Jesus. As Peter went over again and again the tragic happenings of those days, two sayings of our Saviour must have been like rays of light in utter darkness. Our Lord had said at the last supper: "Simon, Simon, behold, Satan hath desired to have you that he may sift you (all) as wheat: But I have prayed for *thee*, that thy faith fail not; AND when thou art CONVERTED (turned again), strengthen thy brethren", Luke 22. 31, 32. The Lord had told him he "would turn again", and had bidden him *strengthen the others*. Why? The Lord had foreseen the temptation, had foreseen the denial, had prophesied his repentance and sorrow, and his restoration to a very great work for Him—to "strengthen" his fellow-workers, be a spiritual help to them. What a comfort this must have been to Peter.

Rest assured that if you are kindly and loving to a fallen brother YOU will be strengthened.

But we have not, even yet, reached the full "height" of the love of God. The risen Saviour had appeared to Mary Magdalene, but not one of the apostles had yet seen Him. They might well have a little doubt about the woman's report. Then some time on that resurrection day Simon Peter saw the Lord Jesus standing by his side. Do you grasp all that it means? The Lord's mother and the other apostles had only heard rumours, and did not see the risen Saviour till late the same evening, about eight o'clock, Luke 24. 34. Yet Peter, who denied that he ever knew Him, and then forsook Him—*this* man is chosen to be the first *man* to see the risen Master! The moment the Saviour vanished from his sight he must have run as he never ran before, to tell the other apostles, "I have seen the Lord!" "He has forgiven me!" All his remorse, and dejection, and shrinking from his old friends had gone. What a welcome back into the fold he received! How they must have envied Peter! He had seen the risen Lord! They probably spent their time together in the upper room talking about nothing else. What had Christ said? What had He done? And when two other disciples knocked at the door late that night, they were greeted with the glad news from the lips of the excited group: "The LORD is risen indeed, and hath APPEARED TO SIMON", Luke 24. 34. "The love of Christ which passeth knowledge", Eph. 3. 19. If ever a man had, in fullest measure, "Joy unspeakable and full of GLORY", it was Simon Peter on the day of the resurrection. How he must have "strengthened the brethren" on that day of gladness.

And *this* is the apostle who taught his converts to love Christ Jesus "with JOY unspeakable and full of GLORY", 1 Pet. 1, 8.

The greatness of God's love can never be measured. Let us never forget that God has done, *and is still* doing, everything that it is possible to do to reveal His love to us. God is LOVE, and the Holy Spirit fills us with hope, "because the love of God is shed abroad in our hearts by the Holy Ghost which is given unto us", Rom. 5. 5. He longs for every man to come to a personal knowledge of that love. There is *another* way in which Christ anticipated Peter's denial, and the dejection and sorrow that followed—even the probability of being "despised" by the other disciples, and perhaps rejected by those amongst whom he had been a leader.

Simon Peter knew the Scriptures. Christ had taught him. You will remember that on the day of the resurrection the risen Lord spent hours in opening up the Scriptures—first to two obscure disciples on the road to Emmaus, making their "hearts burn" within them; and then again in the upper room to the apostles and others, where "He opened their understanding" of things "written in the law of Moses, and in the Prophets and in the Psalms concerning" him, Luke 24. 32, 44, 45. He had been doing that for three years. Six times in the Gospel records we read of His telling how He would be "despised and rejected of men", Isa. 53. 3.

Do you not think that Simon Peter, in his sorrow, remembered that our Lord had suffered such despite although *He* deserved *none* of it? Would not St. Peter get great comfort from the verses which followed: "Surely he hath borne *our* griefs, and carried *our* sorrows . . .

8

wounded for *our* transgressions, . . . bruised for *our* iniquities . . . and with His stripes WE ARE HEALED . . . the Lord hath laid on Him the iniquity of us all", Isa. 53. 4-6. This must have been of great comfort to the lonely apostle in his penitence and sorrow. Simon Peter wrote out of his own experience: "The Lord knoweth how to deliver the godly out of temptations", 2 Pet. 2. 9.

> "Jesus knows all about our sorrows,
> He will guide till our life is done;
> There's not a friend like the lowly Jesus:
> No, not one.

There is yet another striking proof of the love of Jesus for Simon Peter and for us all. We refer to that morning when our Lord stood on the shore of the Sea of Galilee, after a few of His disciples had spent a whole and fruitless night fishing, John 21. 15-22.

After their early meal on the sea shore, our Lord took Simon Peter along the beach for a quiet personal talk. St. John, eager to hear what the Saviour was saying, followed behind, ver. 20. (Did he overhear the conversation, or did Peter confide in him afterwards?) There were no recriminations. No exhortations to be more careful in the future. No reference to the apostle's denial. Just three questions—or rather, *one* question three times asked. "Simon"—not Peter the "rockman"—"Simon, son of Jonas, LOVEST thou Me?" And thrice Peter replies, "Yea, Lord, Thou knowest that I love Thee." That was all, and his Lord gave him a threefold work to do. (1) "Feed My lambs." The man who cursed and swore and lied, and denied the One Who loved him so dearly, is now commissioned to teach children. (2) "Feed My sheep." Teach the grown ups. (3) "TEND My sheep." Instruct them fully in holiness of life. Then, for the *third* time, He said to Peter: "Follow thou Me", Matt. 4. 19; Luke 5. 11.

And if any beloved follower of the Lord Jesus, any Christian worker who has fallen into some conspicuous sin, should read these lines, let him take heart again. The loving Saviour, at all events, will never despair of you, or reject you, if you can truly say, "Yea, Lord, Thou knowest that I LOVE Thee". He will reinstate you, and call you to more devoted service than you have ever known before.

THE PROBLEM OF FALLEN SAINTS!

Some earnest Christian workers are seriously puzzled over the question of great saints, *true saints, ever* falling. They wonder why God had *used* them, and uses them so greatly and in such prominent positions, seeing that He Himself, with His knowledge of the future, foreknew their imminent *fall*.

You may have felt the same difficulty. Why does God bless a man's ministry, or inspire him to write wonderful books, and preach such gracious and helpful sermons, when He knows this saint will fall into grievous sin? And that is a very wise question to ask. The answer to it concerns every one of us, and needs very careful thought and *personal application*. There are three reasons.

(1) It is a *warning* to us all. Such men are our examples. Many of the great saints whose lives are recorded in the Scriptures fell into grievous sins. "These things happened unto them for ensamples", 1 Cor. 10. 5, 6, 11. If such truly saintly men can slip and fall, how careful the rest of us—yes, and the *best* of us—should be! "Wherefore let him that thinketh he standeth, take heed lest he fall", ver. 12. "There hath no temptation taken you, but such as is common to man: but God is faithful, Who will not suffer you to be tempted above that ye are able; but will with the temptation also make a way of escape, that ye may be able to bear it", 1 Cor. 10. 13.

There is the *warning*. If a great saint can fall, how careful the "rank and file" of us must be. I will thank the Lord for giving me warning.

(2) As a *comfort* to us all. Do not misunderstand this.

It should be no comfort to me that when I sin, others are in the same category. Perhaps my example——?

My meaning is this: Christ Jesus has no favourites. He loves us dearly—*all* of us, "saints" and sinners. But never forget that the same Saviour who prayed for all his disciples, yet prayed specially for boastful Simon Peter, *is praying for you and me.* "I have prayed for THEE, that the faith fail not", Luke 22. 32. "He ever liveth to make intercession for us." "Wherefore He is able to save them to the uttermost that come unto God by Him", Heb. 7. 25. The recollection of the Saviour's word must have been an enormous comfort to Simon Peter after his lamentable fall. And it should be a very great comfort to us.

"All have sinned, and come short of the GLORY of God", Rom. 3. 23. "And the Lord hath laid on HIM the iniquity of us all", Isa. 53. 6. And He is praying for *me*: interceding for me; and "He is able to save".

But *now* the Holy Spirit has been poured out upon us, "upon all flesh", Acts 2. 17, 18. And the "Spirit helpeth our infirmities". "The Spirit itself maketh intercession for us with groanings that cannot be uttered: He maketh intercession for the saints according to the will of God", Rom. 8. 26-27.

"Cannot be uttered"! Prayers of such earnestness and yearning that they cannot be expressed in words. Like some of our prayers—so urgent, so vital, so earnest that they reach the very heart of the Saviour before they reach our lips. So "the Spirit helpeth our infirmities, for we know not what to pray for as we ought", ver. 26.

Have you "fallen"? (So have we all.) But you have not fallen from *grace*. Christ has "prayed for THEE, that thy faith fail not".

"Grace there is my every debt to pay,
    Blood to wash my every sin away,
    Power to *keep me holy* day by day,
        In Christ for me."

(3) As a *test*. This test is for all the friends of the fallen saints. We have already referred to that. It is one of the greatest and gravest tests to which any devoted and consecrated man can be put. What is to be our attitude to the fallen saint? What action are we to take? So much depends upon this. Our own spiritual life may be seriously affected; our very souls may be stained by a "holier than thou" attitude. We cannot condone the *sin*; but we can do much to comfort, and sustain, and encourage the sinner. He is far more sorry than we are. Shall we dare to treat him with unveiled contempt? Is any letter we write him—if indeed we relax our condemnation enough to pen him a letter—cold and curt and (to be quite truthful) utterly *unchristian*?

Why, if this is the case, we ourselves have at once "fallen". Or do we immediately write him a kindly, loving, sympathetic, understanding note, assuring him of our love, and sympathy, and sorrow, with perhaps a P.S., "Once a friend always a friend". "Who shall lay anything to the charge of God's elect? It is God that justifieth. *Who is he* that condemneth? It is Christ . . . EVEN AT THE RIGHT HAND OF GOD, Who also maketh intercession for us"—even for the "fallen" Christian, Rom. 8. 33, 34. And—thank God—even for the censorious, "holier-than-thou" Christian.

When the best Bible students—experts in "religion"—condemned a poor sinful woman, the Saviour of the world, Whom the Scriptures "speak of" and reveal, said to her, "Neither do I condemn thee", John 8. 11. (The Bible experts had quietly withdrawn, humbled and convicted.)

If only we can embrace with the arms of love our dear comrade who has "fallen", we may be recalling him to a work like that of Simon Peter, who became so devoted to his Lord and Saviour that (as we pointed out before) the weeping penitent also became so full of the Holy Spirit that he not only loved his Saviour "with joy unspeakable and full of glory", but led his converts to do the same.

There is, however, a TEST also for the "fallen". He is apt to be very sensitive and touchy, and to regard his old friends, but now "cold" friends, with feelings of bitterness. Even if these "friends" are cold and distant, as we put it, and magnify your offence, you must not be annoyed and despise them for their unkind attitude. Dear fallen saint, the Lord Jesus *loves* YOU, and if you are really penitent—as I am quite sure you are—you will love even the bitterest of your old comrades. The Lord said, "Love your enemies", so you *can* love your "cold" friends. "Do good to them that *hate* you." "Pray for them. . . ." And pray for yourself that God will "renew a right spirit within *you*", Psa. 51. 10, to enable you to be a blessing to those who despise you.

If the Saviour could say to Simon Peter, who had enjoyed the inestimable and priceless experience of living for three years with the Son of God and *then* fell, He surely says to you, as a *promise* and a commission: "When thou hast turned again STRENGTHEN THY BRETHREN". *Your greatest work is before you.*

"Be still and know that I am God", or, as Luther translates it: "Be still and *let him mould thee*". *Your* test then becomes an incentive.

May we all have "a heart at leisure from itself to soothe and sympathise". "Be strong in the Lord", Eph. 6. 10.

> "Lord, speak to me, that I may speak
>   In living echoes of Thy tone;
> As Thou hast sought, so let *me* seek
>   Thy erring children lost and *lone*.
>
> "O strengthen me, that while I stand
>   Firm on the rock, and STRONG IN THEE,
> I may stretch out a loving hand
>   To wrestlers with the troubled sea."

God can do anything with a broken heart, provided He has all the pieces.

Chapter XIV

Did Run Well

WE have already spoken about *our* attitude to saints who fall in the race of life. But what is God's attitude to such? Has God no further use for them, and are they to be banished into oblivion? A good look into the life of one of them will answer such questions, and also be the greatest revelation of God's infinite love for all of us. Look at David. How does God speak of the shepherd lad? "The Lord hath sought Him a man after His own heart", 1 Sam. 13. 14. David, we are told, was "a man of a beautiful countenance, and goodly to look to: a comely person, and the Lord was with him", 1 Sam. 16. 12, 18. What more could anyone desire? Yet David fell into very grievous sin: all the more terrible because of his exalted state.

Here is a man chosen, when a shepherd lad, to become one day king. Yet this did not turn his head. As a youth he became the champion and deliverer of Israel, against a giant blasphemer of Jehovah. From our earliest days he has been our favourite Bible character. His beautiful spirit won the loyalty and the deepest affection of the crown prince Jonathan, whom he was to oust from becoming king. Then suddenly, and almost without warning, the whole picture is marred. This idol of our childhood falls into most grievous sins. With well-thought-out subtlety, he betrays the simple-minded captain of his army, and successfully plans the death of a brave soldier, whose wife he covets.

The "sweet singer of Israel", whose songs of praise bore him, as on angels' wings, up to the very gates of heaven, is hustled by one dreadful fall into the dark depths of deceit and adultery and murder. Strange as all this is, yet every one of us may well exclaim: "But for the grace of God, *there go I*". But stranger still is the fact that the Word of God dares to put before us in black and white, the faults and failures, as well as the excellencies and virtues, of its heroes. It relates the half-truths of Abraham, the impatience of Moses, the despondency of Elijah, the cowardice of Peter. And are we not deeply grateful to God that He has done this? It makes us realise that they were all men of "like passions" with ourselves; struggling as we struggle, tempted as we are tempted. The experience of David is the *heart* experience of every Christian. But happy are we if we can truly cry with David: "My soul thirsteth for God", Psa. 42. 2.

Now it is more than likely that some may read this who *did* run well, but were "overtaken in a fault", as we say. Well, what are your feelings? What is to be your attitude to life now? Because of a sudden crash your reputation has been wrecked, your work marred, and possibly your character is "lost". The respect and the sympathy of most of your friends have gone; and even the Christian fellowship with your former Christian friends may be at once withdrawn. To get the "cold shoulder", and, worse still, the cold heart, of those who once loved you, is almost unbearable. (Perhaps they sometimes read what the loving Saviour said about "the first stone", John 8. 7.)

Well, do not think about *their* attitude; if you do so it will only rankle in your heart. But offer up a loving prayer for them in your sorrow for causing their distress of mind. The *great* question for us to ask is: "What is GOD's plan for me? *Has* He a plan for me, or am I cast off for ever?" My own opinion might count for nothing.

It is, however, a very great joy to point to King David's experience. *There* is the answer.

Quite apart from David, the Bible is full of words of forgiveness, of consolation, and comfort: words of cheer and encouragement, and of exceeding great and precious promises, even to sinners. How often we are bidden to forget the things that are behind, not to brood over past failures, but to "press toward the mark for the prize of the high calling of God (*i.e.* the *upward* call) in Christ Jesus", Phil. 3. 13, 14.

The Saviour knows the depth of your sorrow and despair, the genuineness of your repentance, and your eagerness to make amends for giving the enemy occasion to blaspheme, and for giving your *friends* the grave temptation to despise you. God's great LOVE is never seen so "great" as when He is forgiving the sins of all who *love* Him.

We cannot fall away from grace. Christ came to save to the uttermost and He is able to do it. Heb. 7. 24, 25. St. Peter proclaims: "HIM hath God exalted with His right hand to be a Prince and a Saviour". For what purpose? Why? "For to GIVE repentance . . . and forgiveness (remission) of sins", Acts 5. 31.

So come back to King David. "A man after God's own heart." Even such a man fell into very grievous sin. God thereupon sent Nathan, a prophet, to tell him God's judgment upon him. David at once cried out, "I have sinned!" Immediately the answer came, "The Lord also hath put away thy sin", 2 Sam. 12. 13. And *then*? It is this that we wish to emphasize. What was David's next step? What *ought* he to do? Resign his kingship and retire into private life? Write no more Psalms? Not pose any longer as a God-fearing man?

Had he acted thus, and avoided meeting his fellows,

his own realm would have suffered greatly. Nay, more than this, the whole company of the saints in all succeeding generations the wide world over, would have suffered irreparable loss, for who is without sin among us?

What, then, should he do? God had put away his sin. But David is not satisfied even with the declaration of a prophet. In the depth of his great sorrow and remorse, he poured out his heart to God in the privacy of his palace, *for forgiveness*. But he did much more than this. He even let it be widely known throughout the whole kingdom the manner in which he had sought the forgiveness of God, and had found mercy and "grace to help in time of need". Then he went beyond this in his complete confidence in God's love for him, a great sinner. *He prayed to be used as never before*, and to be blessed with all spiritual blessings.

A priest in those days would have been quite content if David had sacrificed a few bullocks! Not so, David. He went away to God and confessed his sin in a prayer which might well have come out of the New Testament. We find it in Psa. 51. Lest your Bible is not close at hand, let us repeat a little of it:

"Have mercy upon me, O God, according to Thy lovingkindness: according to the multitude of Thy tender mercies *blot out* my transgressions. Wash me throughly from mine iniquity, and cleanse me from my sin. For I acknowledge my transgressions. . . .

"Behold Thou desirest truth in the inward parts. . . . Wash me and I shall be whiter than snow. Make me to hear of JOY and GLADNESS. . . . Hide Thy face from my sins, and blot out all my iniquities. Create in me a clean heart, O God; and renew a right spirit within me. Restore unto me the JOY of Thy salvation; and uphold me with Thy free Spitit. Then will I teach transgressors Thy ways; and *sinners shall be converted unto Thee*, . . . and my tongue shall sing aloud of Thy righteousness. . . . O

Lord, open Thou my lips and my mouth shall shew forth Thy praise", Psa. 51.

We question if any man either before or after David has ever been inspired to utter such a contrite, humble and *confident* prayer. He is sure God is willing to *use* him, and is as *certain* that God *will* do so. Who among us has not used David's prayer? It has been an untold blessing to countless generations of *sinners*! And it has also been the prayer on the lips of all the most *saintly* men who ever lived.

For the nearer we draw by faith to the "Light of the World", the blacker our shadow appears to us.

You may be saying, "Ah, but I'm not David"! No, but you have the same Saviour, and the same blessed Holy Spirit Who inspired David to pray; and the Spirit of Christ Jesus, Who ever liveth to make intercession for us, and is able to save to the uttermost them that come unto God by Him", Heb. 7. 25. Yes, and the Spirit Who inspired David to record his prayer, and reveal to us the way in which *he* sought forgiveness, restoration, reinstatement, JOY, and GLORY, can do the same for us.

Had St. Peter lived in David's day, he could have truthfully written to the sweet singer of Israel (as he is called): "Jesus Christ, Whom having not seen, ye LOVE... with JOY unspeakable and full of glory".

Do not lose sight of our object in writing so much about David; he is such an outstanding example of the infinite and unfailing nature of God's love, that we are compelled to ponder over it. It would do us all good if we would read carefully, thoughtfully, and prayerfully the 119th Psalm, asking ourselves again and again: "Do *I* love God's law, meditate over it, delight myself in it, as much as did that busy king? Do *I* seek God with my whole heart? Have I such absolute confidence in God's love for ME, and knowledge of all His mercies bestowed upon ME, and such *certain assurance* that God *always* hears and answers prayer, as David had?"

Then remember *how little of God's Word* David knew! We are far better off than David was. For *we* possess the New Testament, with its story of the earthly life of the Lord Jesus, and His love revealed by the Cross and resurrection and the outpouring of the Holy Spirit; and the perfect example of a holy life that He gives us. Yet David, who was not the happy possessor of these, received such revelations of God's love that to read the Psalms is almost like hearing the love-filled messengers of New Testament writings. Yes, King David, in intense gratitude to God for the forgiveness of his sin learned to love Him "with joy unspeakable and full of glory".

Such reflections as the above will throw a new light, to many, upon some of David's Psalms. Look at two or three verses:

"The steps of a good man are ordered by the Lord: and He delighteth in his way. Though he FALL he shall not be utterly cast down: for the Lord upholdeth him with His hand", Psa. 37. 23, 24.

"The Lord upholdeth *all* that fall: and raiseth up *all* those that be bowed down", Psa. 145. 14.

But there is another and a truly wonderful thing to be remembered. In God's infinite wisdom and foreknowledge He had planned that His well-beloved Son, Jesus Christ, should be known as the "Son of David", and should be born in Bethlehem, and that the first heralding of His birth should be made by angels to shepherds who were watching their flocks in the very fields where King David himself was once a care-free shepherd boy. The Lord Jesus comes to "dwell in our hearts by faith", so that we may be "able to stand" in the face of fierce temptation: and yet, if we fall, to restore unto us the *joy* of His salvation. "Oh that men would praise the Lord for His goodness, and for His wonderful works to the children of men", Psa. 107. 8, 15, 21, 31.

> "Though Jesus Christ in Bethlehem
> A thousand times were born,
> Unless He dwells within my heart,
> I am indeed forlorn."

Chapter XV

Jesus Made Manifest

In Our Body

IT is the life that tells more than the lip. But with our lips we *must* witness for Christ. Do you find it difficult to talk about spiritual things to others? Well, try putting yourself at their feet as a learner. People object to being asked, "Are you saved"? But they feel a bit flattered if the question is put to them: "How long have you known Christ as your Saviour?" Such a question rarely fails to lead up to an intimate chat about the way of salvation, which may be followed up by offering a suitable tract or booklet. But we must be *guided* by the indwelling Christ.

And we must use wisdom. You may have heard of the converted barber, who, in the midst of shaving a man, held up the open razor and said, "Are you ready to die?" The customer disappeared very quickly.

One gets many an opportunity with total strangers. Try it on a "scavenger" (as we used to call men who sweep up the rubbish from the streets). Begin by saying: "My good friend, you're in the Ministry of Health, and worth a dozen doctors! They can *heal* diseases, but you are preventing them". Then say, "Will you do this sort of work in heaven?" One man of whom I asked that question, gave me a radiant smile, and replied, "No, sir! I shall not." "But why not?" "Well," said he "the good Book says, 'There shall in no wise enter into it anything that defileth', Rev. 21. 27. There will be no jobs like this in heaven".

But it is the radiant Christian, the man who lets everything go out of his life that would dim the GLORY Christ offers us, whose witness the world most needs. Please look at a few examples, and carefully note *how* the radiance, the GLORY, came.

CHIANG KAI SHEK

Is it not a truly marvellous and providential thing that the greatest soldier in China, the Generalissimo of the Chinese Army, should be a keen Christian man? How did it come to pass? He was a Buddhist, but married an earnest Christian.

Some years back he was a Communist General, with an army of ruthless cut-throats. One day they attacked an inland city. They killed all who resisted and savagely slaughtered any Christians they could lay hands on. They set fire to the hospital run by an American missionary, and then looted the town.

The General took possession of one of the best houses, and brought his wife with him. At the earliest possible moment the U.S.A. missionary doctor called to see him, and met with a very cold reception.

"Sir", said the doctor, "I've come to ask a favour. I have been doctoring here for thirty years. But now your soldiers have burnt my hospital to the ground. What few patients escaped death have fled. May I be allowed to treat your wounded men?"

Permission was readily granted, and the doctor left. The General told his wife of what, to him, was an extraordinary thing. "I have burnt his hospital, and house, and all he has, and now he wants to heal our wounded!" "No," replied the wife, "it is not at all extraordinary. He is only carrying out the teaching of his religion. Jesus Christ bade his disciples to love their enemies, and to do good to them that despitefully use you".

This so impressed that great soldier that he asked for further teaching, and was in due course baptized. So to-day China has as Generalissimo one of the keenest Christians in that great country.

By that one act—an act which revealed the GLORY Christ gives to consecrated men—the Missionary did a work of far greater value than all the labour of thirty years, for Chiang Kai Shek himself became a great lover of the Doctor's Saviour.

But Chiang Kai Shek was not only truly converted. He became a radiant Christian full of the GLORY. It is only a few years ago that we were startled by an account that appeared in our newspapers of the kidnapping of Chiang Kai Shek. When motoring a few miles outside a city, an aeroplane suddenly swooped down. The General's car was stopped, and he was hustled into the plane and taken prisoner by a rival and hostile army. The only thing he asked to keep was his Bible. But he was allowed permission to send for his wife. Every morning they spent an hour together in studying the Scriptures. The rival General called himself a Communist. He became very suspicious about these long discussions every day. At last he determined to find out what was going on, and asked if he might come every day and listen. In a very short time he accepted Christ as his Saviour and liberated his prisoner, Chiang Kai Shek, who had received the GLORY and passed it on.

H. M. STANLEY

You probably know the story of how Livingstone went out to Central Africa to win the Dark Continent for Christ. For a long time no news came of him—he was lost. But the *New York Herald* sent out H. M. Stanley with orders to find him at whatever cost. He *did* find him, and stayed with him some time. But as Livingstone refused to come home, Stanley returned alone. And this is what he wrote concerning Livingstone:

"Here is a man who is manifestly *sustained* as well as guided by influences from Heaven. The Holy Spirit dwells in him. God speaks through him. The heroism, the nobility, the pure and stainless enthusiasm, the root of his life *came, beyond question*, from Christ. There must, therefore, be a Christ, and it is worth while to have such a Helper and Redeemer as this Christ undoubtedly is, as He *reveals Himself* in this wonderful disciple". Stanley came to have a belief in Christ because he saw Christ's GLORY in the saintly doctor.

It was my privilege to know one of the African natives who helped to carry Livingstone's body down to Mombasa *en route* to be buried in Westminster Abbey. He remained in England. It was evident that the GLORY had been received by *him*. His radiant black face at open-air meetings was a benediction.

THE FACTORY GIRL

We are all so prone to think that God has favourites and He gives His "glory" to a select few. Or we think that there is something in our "make-up" that prevents us from receiving His GLORY. *It is not so.* Any one of us may be "full of His glory", provided we do not keep one little corner of our heart for ourselves.

Let me tell how a most unlikely person became filled with the very glory of God. Some years ago, within the lifetime of many of us, there lived a girl in a Manchester slum. She was brought up in a godless home. One who knew her said to me: "It was a *rotten family*". At fourteen she left school and became a factory hand, working at a loom. When twenty years of age she drifted into a Gospel Hall and was converted. In a little time she fell deeply in love with Christ, and longed to do more for

9

Him, little knowing what an influence her radiant life already had.

She wrote to a Missionary Society asking them to send her to India. They looked at the cheap paper and criticized the spelling, and wrote a kindly letter of refusal. She wrote again, simply to ask one question: "Did you pray for *guidance* in your decision?" No, they had *not* done so, she was so *obviously* unsuitable. So an interview was granted. The committee felt that with her slight education she would never learn a language. But a dear friend of mine, who related the story to me, and who was on that committee (and may still be on it), offered to pay for her education for three years, and then to pay her passage out to India, and also her salary.

In six months she learnt both Urdu and Marathi, and did an unparalleled work, because of the "glory" that shone in her happy radiant face. When she grew older she refused to retire. So my friend insisted on her travelling on a steamer which carried only first-class passengers. When she entered the dining saloon the first evening, crowded as it was with fashionably dressed people—a brilliant company—everybody glanced at her. It was not because of her simple dress, but because of her radiantly happy face.

There was no chaplain on board, so she asked the Captain if she might conduct a service on Sunday. He was completely staggered, but the GLORY on her very face gained the day. The Captain wrote to the Secretary of her Society at the end of the voyage. He said that *all* the passengers came to the service every Sunday. Then he added, "We were all so impressed by the radiance of her religion, that everybody—passengers and crew—sought her out for quiet talks about religion". It was the GLORY that did this great work.

O let us pray, that the eyes of our understanding being enlightened, we may know what is the hope of His calling, and what the riches of the GLORY of His inheritance in the saints." Eph. 1. 18.

A few earnest Christian workers were discussing a well-known and very successful Evangelist. They were wondering wherein lay his success. All agreed that his addresses were not attractive, nor was his method of conveying the truth, or his mode of preaching. Yet there were such wonderful results! At last one of them exclaimed: "I'll tell you what it is. There is nothing IN him to prevent God working *through* him."

"JESUS, when He had called unto Him His twelve disciples, He gave them POWER", Matt. 10. 1.

Let us ask ourselves is there anything in *me* that prevents God working through me? Is there anything in *me* that prevents God using my Vicar, my Pastor, or my colleagues in their daily occupation? A wise old saint said to some theological students: "It is no use walking to preach unless you preach as you walk". "None of us liveth to himself", Rom. 14. 7. A little sinfulness in me, or in you, may ruin a mission or hinder God from using a truly faithful pastor. My belief is that mere "theorising" does little good, so please let me show you my meaning by a story.

ROBERT HARKNESS

There are few men, if any, who have written such soul-stirring, appealing hymns and hymn tunes as Robert Harkness. How did this come about? He met Dr. Torrey, the world-wide evangelist, in Australia and New Zealand, and it is Robert Harkness himself who told this story. Dr. Torrey was advertised to take a ten days' mission at Dunedin, in the largest hall in the town. Harkness was conducting the singing. Night after night the Hall was crowded with eager listeners. But there was no response to Torrey's appeals. Friday evening came—but still no response.

Before dismissing the great audience, Doctor Torrey said: "Everybody who can will meet in the Y.M.C.A. Hall to-night at 11 p.m. for a half-night prayer meeting under the direction of Mr. Harkness". This came as a veritable shock to Harkness. In telling the story, he said: "*I* knew nothing about half-night prayer meetings!" Some 500 people turned up at 11 o'clock, and Harkness came on to the platform. But before he could speak, a man in the audience rose and said: "Mr. Harkness, may I say something?" "By all means," came the answer. Then came this statement: "Sir, I believe that the hindrance to the working of the Holy Spirit is *right here* —in this room. Someone has not made a full surrender to Christ." Then he sat down. There was a long pause. People wondered what would happen. Harkness remained seated and bowed his head upon the table in earnest prayer.

After some time he stood up, and this is what he said: "Will all the praying people here pray for *me*. *I* have never fully surrendered myself to the Lord Jesus. But I do so *now*". The effect was simply astonishing. Scores of people rose one after another to confess to this sin or that, and made full surrender to the Saviour. It was so spontaneous and so sincere.

When Dr. Torrey made his appeal for decision the next day a few hundred people responded to the invitation to accept Christ as their Saviour. One was a young man who had hitherto resisted every appeal, and who now is one of the greatest soul-winners in New Zealand.

CHAPTER XVI

What is Glory?

OUR Lord said to His Heavenly Father, "The GLORY which Thou gavest Me, I have given them"— My disciples, John 17. 22. What was it? What *is* that "glory"? We have already seen that Christ told the Father that He had given Him (Christ Jesus) seven things. Our Lord also tells how that He gave His disciples seven things. So you can see how easy it is to be confused and puzzled as to what this GLORY can be.

Saintly scholars all down the ages have differed upon this important question.

Two things we are *sure of*: (1) "Glory" is something the Father gave to His well-beloved Son, and which the Son has given us. (2) It is something that can be SEEN. Speaking of our Lord, St. John says: "The Word was made flesh and dwelt among us (and we beheld His GLORY, the glory as of the only begotten of the Father) full of grace and truth", John 1. 14.

Glory is the greatest of all Christ's gifts to us; for we *cannot* have this GLORY unless Christ dwells in our hearts by faith, and we are rooted and grounded in LOVE . . . and know the love of Christ that passeth knowledge, Eph. 3. 17-19. How natural it seems for St. Paul to add: "unto Him be GLORY in the Church (*i.e.* all true believers in all the 'churches') by Christ Jesus".

This is the greatest gift God ever made to His Son, and *it is given to us* by our Saviour. But it is all IN Christ. "Christ IN you the hope of GLORY." Glory *here* and glory hereafter.

Seeing there is no greater gift than glory, will you note what the saints and scholars of old have said about it? Their opinions shall be numbered and commented upon after you have thought them over.

(1) Chrysostom: The unity of the Spirit. Eph. 4. 3.

(2) Augustine. The glory of immortality which human nature received of Christ.

(3) Luther. Oneness: the glory of unity.

(4) À. Lapide. The glory of becoming sons of God.

(5) Bengel. The glory of the Only-Begotten shining out through us.

(6) Godet. The LOVE which the Father has to the Son; and which He gives us. The glorious unity of Divine love.

(7) Calvin. The blessedness of having the image of God formed afresh in us. The bringing of the Father's glory into human nature.

(8) Bishop Westcott. The perfect apprehension of the Father as fulfilling His work of love; or the revelation of the Divine in man, realised in and through Christ.

(9) Bishop Moule. The gift of a spiritual and real sonship to God in Christ, based on the "gift" of the Father to the Son of the eternal timeless generation.

Others say it is the Holy Spirit, "the Spirit of Glory", 1 Pet. 4. 14; or the power of working miracles; or "the absolutely perfect personal excellencies of Christ"; or the Holy Communion.

Now if your mind is as simple as mine, I am sure you are utterly bewildered by this time. But when you have thought over those varied opinions of great scholars who were all great saints, just look at them once more and note this about them:

(1) There is no mention of the Holy Spirit in St. John 17, although the Holy Spirit reveals God's gifts and conveys them.

(2) "Immortality" cannot be seen. St. John says, "We beheld His glory".

(3) Unity cannot be "glory"; but "glory" comes out of spiritual unity. Luther was evidently emphasizing verses 21 and 23.

(4) Sons of God? "Now are we sons of God, and it does not yet appear what we shall be", 1 John 3. 2. Yet there are many children of God who reveal very little, or *no* glory.

(5) This is one of the best answers to our question; but *What is the glory?* (that shines through us?) St. Paul prays for his converts, "That the name of our Lord Jesus Christ may be glorified in you, and ye in Him", 2 Thess. 1. 12.

(6) Does not our Lord say that the "glory" is the *outcome* of God's love—not merely the love itself; and that this love comes from Him? The glory *results* from the things spoken of in John 17. 23-26.

(7) What is this "image of God formed in us"? And what is this "GLORY" which comes into human nature?

(8) Bishop Westcott says that "glory" is the revelation of the Divine in man by Jesus Christ. There we come back to St. Paul's statement: *"Christ in you* the hope of glory".

Many other explanations are given by various people.

Now please do not close this book and vow you can read no more, for this GLORY is the gift of God for *you*. And the main purpose of this book is that you should know exactly WHAT THAT GLORY IS; and you should earnestly beseech God to take out of your heart and mind everything that hinders the reception of this inestimable gift. After speaking of "the exceeding grace of God in you", St. Paul adds: "Thanks be unto God for His unspeakable gift", 2 Cor. 9. 15. And we would, like St. Paul, pray for you that you may be full of God's glory, so that St. Peter's words may be true of you: "Jesus Christ Whom, not having seen, ye LOVE with JOY unspeakable and full of GLORY".

One feels so ashamed of one's self to disagree with such saints and men of such scholarship; men—two of them—from whom the writer has received hospitality at a time when he himself was not sufficiently "grown in grace" to talk over these divine truths. But my firm conviction is that the Lord Jesus can reveal to the humblest Christian, and one who has no claim whatever to scholarship, the deepest truths of Scripture.

Did not our Lord *rejoice* in spirit and say, "I thank Thee, O Father, Lord of heaven and earth, that Thou hast hid these things from the wise . . . and hast revealed them unto babes; even so, Father, for so it seemed good in Thy sight"? Luke 10. 21.

May we therefore think over what the "glory" really is, praying that our Saviour will reveal His glory *to* us, and then reveal it *through us* to others. There is no glory apart from Christ. St. Paul says: "His saints to whom God would make known what is the riches of the GLORY . . . which is *Christ in you*, the hope of glory", Col. 1. 27.

Glory in us—the gift of Christ—is just the *out-shining of the in-living Christ*. That is why, after His resurrection, our Saviour told His disciples not to depart from Jerusalem, but to wait for the promise of the Father—the promised Holy Ghost. He said: "Ye shall be baptised with the Holy Ghost not many days hence". "Ye shall receive the power of the Holy Ghost coming upon you", Acts 1. 5, 8 (marg.). When our Lord walked this earth

as a homeless Man, Who "had not where to lay His head",
Luke 9. 58, He said of the Holy Spirit, "the Spirit of
Truth", "He dwelleth *with* you and shall be *in* you",
John 14. 17. That "indwelling" took place on the day
of Pentecost. "They were ALL filled with the Holy
Ghost and began to *speak* . . . as the Spirit gave them
utterance". They spoke about the "wonderful works
of God", Acts 2. 4, 11.

But the Holy Spirit does not "fill" us simply to make us
full of joy, or in order to fill our hearts with love and
gratitude to the Saviour; although He can and will do
this. Our Lord said of Him, "He shall *glorify* Me".
How will He do that? "He shall glorify Me, for He shall
receive of Mine (*take* of mine, R.V.) and shall *shew* it unto
you" (declare it unto you, R.V.), John 16. 14-15.

The Holy Spirit's great work—perhaps His *only* work
is to manifest, reveal, show, and declare all that the
Lord Jesus *is* and *can* be to us. He tells us of Christ's
words of love; He tells us of His *deeds* of love and compassion and power. *He expects us to know our Bibles.*
Our Lord Himself said: "If a man love Me, he will keep
My words: AND My Father will love him, and *we* will
come unto him and make our abode with him. . . . The
Holy Ghost, Whom the Father will send in My name, He
shall teach you all things and bring to your remembrance
whatsoever I have said unto you", John 14. 23-26.

That is the work of God the Holy Spirit: just to glorify
the Lord Jesus. And that is *our* work too. As we begin
each new day we might do well to say aloud:

> "Forth in Thy Name, O Lord, I go,
>   My daily labour to pursue;
> Thee, *only* Thee, resolved to know,
>   In all I think, or say, or do."

But the Holy Spirit cannot "bring to our *remembrance*" things of which we have never heard. If our
Bible is a closed book to us, must not the Holy Spirit

have closed lips oftentimes? He dwells in us, it is true, but may be unable to reveal His messages. He inspired St. Paul to write: "Let the word of Christ dwell in you richly", Col. 3. 16.

Quite early in His ministry on earth our Lord said: "The words that I speak unto you, they are Spirit, and they are LIFE", John 6. 63. And at the close of His ministry He brings to the Father's special notice: "I have given unto them the WORDS which Thou gavest Me, and they have received them", John 17. 8. Is it not true of many Christian people that they would like to pick and choose from amongst the gifts of the Lord Jesus? We all want the joy He gives; we all—*i.e.* all who have given it serious thought—would like to have the "glory"; but how few take any real interest in His *words*? You will never meet a radiant Christian who is not a lover of the Word of God.

Moody said: "When I PRAY, I talk to God. But when I read the Bible, God is talking to me; and it is really more important that God should speak to me, than I to Him".

We have been thinking of the GLORY the Father gave Christ, and have seen that the glory was the revealing, the revelation, manifestation, of God the Father's nature or "name". Everything about Christ was an unveiling of the love of God the Father for us. He showed us what God is like. He did this so perfectly, so clearly, that He could truthfully declare, "He that hath seen *Me*, hath seen the Father", John 14. 9. His glory was radiant holiness; but His glory was, at the same time, God's *love* revealed.

You may at once reply: "'But I am not God, and *I* can never say, He that hath seen Me hath seen the Father'. We *dare not say* such a thing". But Christ

clearly promised that the Holy Spirit, Who is God,
should be sent to dwell *in* us. "He dwelleth with you",
said our Lord, "and shall be *in you*", John 14. 17. Now
the Holy Spirit, like our Saviour, cannot "be hid",
Mark 7. 24. *He will "manifest" the Saviour.* Our Lord
said, "He will take of Mine and shall show it unto you",
John 16. 15. But He will not be content with showing
Christ to us. He desires to enable us, and to inspire us,
to take of Christ's—the things of Christ, and show them
to others. Yes, and *declare* them to others. And that is
THE GLORY GIVEN TO US.

When we are wholly yielded up to our loving, heavenly
Father, and desire to be always "to the praise of the
GLORY of His grace", Eph. 1. 6, our Saviour will see to
it that *His* glory, which He gives us, will be manifested—
made seen—in us. And that is why we were chosen in
Him before the foundation of this earth, Eph. 1. 4. But it
will *always* be, "Christ in you the hope of glory", Col. 1. 27.

Why do we not *see* this? Why do we not seek to know
all it involves? How did our Lord show forth this glory?
Listen to His own explanation: "I do nothing of Myself;
but as My Father hath taught Me, I speak these things.
And He that sent Me is with Me: the Father hath not left
Me alone; for I DO ALWAYS THOSE THINGS THAT PLEASE
HIM", John 8. 28-29. Our business in life is to "run the
race set before us, looking unto Jesus", Heb. 12. 1-2.
He dwells within us, our constant Companion, and
Friend, and Guide, and Lover; and through HIM and
His love and power and guidance we also, "whether we
eat or drink or whatsoever we do, may do all to the
GLORY of God".

Such a life is perfect freedom, because it is a God-
guided life, and a God-empowered life. Christ Jesus
dwelling in us would still say, "The Father hath not left
Me alone". Do you remember what we said earlier in
the book? The Lord Jesus will never ask us to *do* any-

thing that is not for our highest good. He will never *withhold from us* anything that it is good for us to have. He will give us strength to obey all His commands. And if any one of us wrote out a scheme for the happiest and best life we think we could possibly choose and plan for ourselves, we may be absolutely certain that God has marked out for us something better. Talk these things over with fellow-Christians. Meditate on them on your knees and ask Christ's clear guidance for "manifesting forth the glory".

> "Make me a captive, Lord,
>   And then I shall be free;
> Force me to render up my sword,
>   And I shall conqueror be.
> I sink in life's alarms
>   When by myself I stand;
> Imprison me within Thine arms,
>   And STRONG shall be my hands."

CHAPTER XVII

The Gifts of God

WE have already called your very special attention to St. John 17, the most wonderful of all utterances ever made. Have you noticed that it is a very remarkable chapter of GIFTS? They are the gifts of the everlasting Father to the everlasting Son, when His Son "was made flesh, and dwelt among us", and men beheld His GLORY. When you recall the fact that "all things were made by Him"—*i.e.* the Lord Jesus—you may well ask: "Then what else can the Father *give* Him?" But our astonishment knows no bounds when we find that our Saviour *bestows many of these gifts on us.* God said to His people of old, "Thou hast despised Mine holy things", Ezek. 22. 8. What does God think of us if we despise or ignore His great and gracious gifts or the riches of His goodness? Rom. 2. 4. What are these gifts?

GOD THE FATHER GAVE TO CHRIST JESUS seven things.

(1) Power to give eternal life. ver. 2.

(2) The Saviour's *work* on earth. ver. 4.

(3) The words that He should speak to us. verses 8, 13, 14.

(4) His commission—*i.e.* His sending from heaven to earth. God sent His Son. ver. 18.

(5) Power to manifest, that is, *reveal* God's name, character, nature: revealing God to man as *Saviour*. vers. 6, 26.

(6) The Father gave us MEN to His Son—you and me. *We* are a gift of God the Father to Christ Jesus. Seven times our Lord refers to that GIFT. verses 2, 6 (twice), 9, 11, 12, 24.

(7) Glory. ver. 22.

WHAT CHRIST GIVES US. Seven things.

Our gracious God and Father said in Isaiah's day,

"Put Me in remembrance", Isa. 43. 26. Here we find our Lord doing this to His Father. He "reminds" Him of the gifts that He, the beloved Son, has made to us—to YOU and to ME, John 17. 20. What are they?

(1) Eternal life. ver. 2. Read John 20. 31: "These things are written that ye might believe that Jesus is the Christ, the Son of God, and that believing ye might have life through His name".

(2) His love. ver. 26.

(3) His joy. ver. 13.

(4) His words. vers. 8, 13. 14.

(5) *Our* commission—our "sending forth". ver. 8.

(6) His prayers. vers. 9, 20; cp. Luke 11. 1.

(7) Power to manifest, show forth, REVEAL to others Christ as Saviour by our *words* and life. That is GLORY. ver. 22.

Think over these wonderful gifts; pray over them. Look again at verse 20: "Neither pray I for these alone, but for them also which shall believe on Me *through their word*". Do you see the wonder of it? There were men living in Jerusalem and all over Judea and Galilee who had heard the Saviour speak, and had seen His miracles and had watched His life, but who went away unbelieving. Yet by the words of those apostles many of these would come to accept Christ as their Saviour.

We read that very soon after our Lord's resurrection, as a result of the preaching of the apostles and their converts, "a great company of the priests were obedient to the faith", Acts 6. 7. Is *this* what our Lord was thinking of when He said: "He that believeth on Me, the works that I do shall he do also; and GREATER works than these shall he do, because I go to the Father"? John 14. 12. It may be. But one fact stands out clearly, and that is that the Saviour expects *us* who love Him to *witness* for Him to others and to be "fishers of men".

CHAPTER XVIII

How Revivals Come

A VERY little mist hides the glory of the sun, and a very little sin in the life prevents God's glory being revealed in us. Fifteen years ago it was my privilege to conduct a little convention in a town in South Wales. Arriving at Paddington Station, I was glad to secure an empty compartment, so as to have a quiet time in prayer and meditation. The guard held his whistle to his lips, waiting to signal our departure, when suddenly my carriage door was flung open, and a voice cried, "Is this seat reserved?" "Yes", was my quick reply, "it is reserved for *you*. Come in, and welcome!"

But he was an absolute stranger to me. Why, then, this glad welcome? Simply because he had such a *radiantly happy face*. "I see we are kindred spirits," he exclaimed. I soon learnt that he was the owner of a great London emporium—a veritable "Whiteley's"— and was running down to Wales for Sunday Services in a big chapel, and was returning to London on Monday. "No," I replied, "you will come back on Thursday, please, and we will travel back together". This, he assured me, was impossible—business could not be neglected. We had a delightful time together, and parted company at Cardiff. On Thursday morning I was on the Cardiff platform awaiting my train, when my friend with the radiant face arrived! Why had he stayed till Thursday? This was his story:

On Sunday morning the Chapel was quite full, but I was not happy about it. My sermon seemed cold and dull; the people seemed quite unresponsive. In the evening every available place was occupied—pulpit steps, window sills, and every bit of standing room. But God was not working. I felt it. I *knew* it.

At last I broke off my address and told the people my sorrow, and asked them to be silent in prayer for me. Then suddenly two men stood up. They looked at one another and then turning toward me, one of them said: "*I* am to blame. I quarrelled with Brother So-and-so eight months ago over the date on which we should hold the Sunday School annual treat. We have not spoken to each other since."

The other man said: "No, sir, it's all *my* fault. God forgive me." The men pushed their way to the aisle and shook hands heartily. "Then," said my friend in the train, "I continued my little talk, but there was no need for any further exhortation. People broke down all over the building, and such a blessing followed that they pleaded with me to conduct services through the week. And now I've left them to carry on the mission which was so strangely forced upon us."

Men have often told me that their Vicar or Pastor was a failure. They say there are no conversions, and they themselves get no help from his ministry. But may not the blame be on the critics? Are they themselves responsible for the lack of blessing? Have they quarrelled over something even more trivial than the date of the Sunday School treat?

One saddened Vicar told me that the wives of his two Churchwardens were not on *speaking* terms with each other. I asked a wholly consecrated man, and therefore one much used of God, how he came into the fullness of blessing. He said it was because he was asked to address a gathering of ministers on holiness and full surrender to Christ. In the middle of his address the Holy Spirit convicted him of speaking beyond his own experience.

He felt so confused and uneasy that he hesitated, then stood speechless. The chairman, an elderly Baptist minister, and a dear child of God, saw what was the matter, and turning to the speaker, thanked him for his address. Then he added, "Let us pray". While they prayed, my friend quietly slipped out of the hall and hastened home. There he fell on his knees sobbing. He pleaded for forgiveness and yielded himself entirely to God. And now his ministry is blessed wherever he goes.

Remember that even the most humble and obscure Christian may exercise a powerful influence for good. You probably know the story of Peter Mathison, who was Sir Walter Scott's most trusted servant. He was a devoutly religious man, and exercised a great spiritual influence over Sir Walter. It was Peter's custom to finish the day with family worship in his little home. Scott was most anxious to share that worship. He went to great trouble, and exercised much ingenuity in providing a secret and unusual provision for overhearing his gardener's prayers—his intimate conversation with his beloved Saviour. It was Sir Walter's custom to steal down in the evening to Peter Mathison's cottage and listen to his servant communing with his heavenly Master. We all know the wide influence of Sir Walter Scott's books, but we cannot measure how much of it is due to Peter's holy life and prayers.

Even little children can be a real and mighty power for God. Five years ago a Chinese girl of twelve years old was withdrawn from a Mission School, where she was a boarder. Her parents said she must now earn her living, and be sent to a city thirty miles away to work in a heathen home. She came to the room of the lady missionary to say good-bye. Then turning round once more she said quietly, "I shall be the only Christian in the city".

10

"Yes," replied the missionary, "but you know Who is going with you?" "O yes," said the little child, her face lighted up with joy, "The Lord Jesus Christ".

In that heathen city the small Christian refused to worship idols or do reverence to the household gods; and, as a result, was not a little persecuted. She showed no resentment, but was always sweet and kindly whatever they said or did. A month or two later, two men walked those thirty miles and called at the Mission School. They said they were sent to ask if the Christians would send someone to teach them about Jesus and start a school.

Now the missionaries had several times tried to get permission to work in that city, but always in vain. "Why do you ask us to do this?" she said. Their reply was that a little girl of twelve had come to the city, and everyone who visited the house where she worked, was struck by her happy radiant face, and gentle, kindly manner. When questioned about it, she would reply it was because she loved Jesus and He loved her and was always with her. "We want the other girls in our city to become like that Christian girl," they added. One little radiant Christian child opened up a hostile city for the Gospel message.

"I am not a Christian—far from it," said a Doctor to me. "But there's one thing: I never swear or use bad language when my young brother of fourteen is present. He is such a bright Christian laddie, that I would rather cut my tongue out than injure his faith or his love for Jesus."

One who is very dear to me went out to India to visit missions. He came to a village—almost a *town*—where many "untouchables", *outcasts* who are supposed to have no souls—had become Christians. My friend asked the heathen priest there: "Is there any difference between these out-caste Christians and the heathen?"

"Difference!" replied the priest, "*all the difference in the world*. The Christians are as different from the other people as noonday is from midnight and heaven from earth."

What are you going to do about this matter? Face the question we *implore* you. Are YOU fully yielded up to Christ to do His will? Our lives are *short* enough. What about the prayer-life? What about devotional study of the Bible, and meditating over it in the presence of God? Is there any quarrel or unpleasantness that needs putting right? Never was there a time when Radiant Christians were so needed or so welcomed. For the sake of the *Saviour* "Who loved us and gave Himself for us", for the sake of your family and friends, for your minister and fellow-worshippers, and for your own sake, we *beseech* you put all you are and have wholly at Christ's disposal. "We are ambassadors for Christ, as though GOD did beseech you by us: we *pray* you in Christ's stead, BE YE RECONCILED TO GOD", 2 Cor. 5. 20.

CHAPTER XIX

Easy Yokes

WHY is it that so few of us are willing to yield our-selves wholly into the hands of Christ, gladly and joyously to obey His every known command, and diligently to search our Bibles to discover His will for us? The devil does his utmost to lead us to mistrust and distrust our loving Heavenly Father. We *profess* to believe that the Scriptures are the Word of God and yet——? May it be that we do not trust God wholly and fully because we do not know our Bibles sufficiently? Or is it because we think *we* know how to run our lives better than *God* knows?

Three great and outstanding facts are in my mind. They cannot be denied, and they can be proved by the sure warrant of Scripture.

(1) God *demands* of us nothing that can or will harm us. *Never!* We cannot find in Scripture any command of God that will harm us or injure us in body, soul, or spirit, if we obey it. Nay, more. There is nothing asked of us but what will be for our eternal benefit and everlasting good. Our earthly life will be more happy, more joyous, more fruitful the more willingly we obey all God's commandments. My firm belief is that our joy in heaven will be greater if our obedience on earth is more complete. Listen to God's promise once more. If we are but *willing* and *obedient*, then God makes this truly glorious promise:

"I will REJOICE over thee to do thee good . . . *assuredly* with My WHOLE HEART and with My WHOLE SOUL", Jer. 32. 41.

Now that is God's word. That is God's promise. We

cannot conceive of any greater blessing that God could give us. God is love, and God will never harm us or allow anything to befall us that will not be for our highest and eternal good.

(2) Then nothing will be *denied* us that would be a real blessing to us. Nothing!

"They that seek the Lord shall NOT WANT ANY GOOD THING", Psa. 34. 10.

Does not the promise still stand true:

"No GOOD THING will He withhold from them that walk uprightly"? Psa. 84. 11.

We shall not have any less pleasure, any less JOY, any less peace of mind and heart if we follow Christ Jesus wholly. We may have to give up some doubtful habit or attitude which appears to *us* as very desirable. But it is absolutely certain that God denies to His children nothing that would really be for our advantage. He prays that His joy may be in us, and that *our* joy may be full; and we know that He asks only those things that please Him—our loving Heavenly Father.

Sit down for a few minutes and think over the kind of life you would like to live; and the things you would like to have—*the best* possible life you can conceive. Then—*even then*—you can be certain that the life God is fashioning for you is infinitely better than the life you have sketched out for yourself. For God "is able to do exceeding abundantly above all that we ask or THINK" Eph. 3. 20.

Life—life "more abundant"—is the life God has planned for us, and promises to give to all who will accept it. That was His purpose in coming down to dwell on earth. Not only to "leave us an example that we should follow His steps", 1 Pet. 2. 21; but also to show us "His steps". "Life more abundantly" is the life God intends man to have, and has made man capable of receiving and enjoying. Its source is in Christ. Its food is His fellowship. Its duration is eternal. And since this is the life which will be lived in heaven, where we all desire to go one day, is it not the most enjoyable life that God Himself can devise for us? Why then do we hesitate in accepting it? Then we stand up and sing heartily:

> "I dare not choose my lot,
> I would not if I might.
> Choose Thou for me my God,
> So shall I walk aright."

God *has* chosen. "For we know that ALL things work together for good to them that love God, to them who are the called according to His PURPOSE", Rom. 8. 28. St. Paul, to whom this great truth was revealed, had proved it for himself. And God gave him a promise for all others:

> "My God shall supply all your NEED, according to His riches in GLORY, by Christ Jesus", Phil. 4. 19.

(3) Then remember that God has promised that His strength shall be given us to enable us to do all that He commands us to do. We never *need* fail. "As thy days so shall THY strength be", Deut. 33. 25.

Now, if only all true followers of the Lord Jesus would believe those three immutable facts stated above, and would live in such a way as to show to all others around that they trusted the Saviour implicitly and unwaveringly, a great revival would break out. But, alas, *so few*— so very few—are Christians of this sort.

No doubt many reading this will cry: But "who is sufficient for these things"? 2 Cor. 2. 16. Sufficient? Why, it is not *our* "sufficiency" which can avail us in temptation or difficulty, or distress. Did not St. Paul tell us so? "Not that we are sufficient of ourselves to think anything as of ourselves (*i.e. to account anything as from ourselves*, R.V.), but our sufficiency is of GOD", 2 Cor. 3. 5. The Apostle Paul is so absolutely certain of this fact, proved by his own experience, that he says it over and over again. "And God IS ABLE to make all grace abound unto you, that ye, having ALWAYS all-sufficiency in every thing, may abound unto every good work", 2 Cor. 9. 8. But He is not only *able*, He is *willing*, and He has pledged Himself to do so. When God allowed that "thorn (*stake*) in the flesh", Paul prayed thrice for it to be taken away. And Christ Himself, the glorified and reigning Christ, said to Paul: "My grace is sufficient for thee: for My strength (*power*) is made perfect in weakness", 2 Cor. 12. 9. And he believed God: and he came to GLORY in his "weakness" or infirmities. Why? He tells us "That the power of Christ may rest upon me", (or *cover me*, R.V., margin).

> "God hath not promised skies ever blue,
> Flower-strewn pathways always for you.
> God hath not promised sun without rain,
> Joy without sorrow, peace without pain.
> But He hath promised STRENGTH FROM ABOVE,
> Unfailing sympathy, undying love."

Do you not consider those three unalterable *facts* concerning God and His loving purposes for us sufficient to lead us to put our whole trust in Him? If my own heart and conscience did not condemn me for failing oft-times to act up to my belief, I should thimk that with such promises from God's own lips, it would be impossible for us to act as if we could plan our own lives in a better way than God purposes to do, or to grumble or murmur when things *seem to us* to go wrong.

Truly, it is JOY unspeakable to yield one's self wholly to such a Saviour and Friend.

Ever remember that in the service of God, strength sufficient for any task, patience to bear any suffering, courage to face any danger or peril, will ALWAYS be given us. Moreover, "He is able to do exceeding abundantly above all that we ask or think", Eph. 3. 20.

CHAPTER XX

Ye Should Follow His Steps

"WE should follow His steps." That is what Simon Peter says in his First Epistle. "Christ also suffered for us, leaving us an example, that ye should follow His steps", 1 Pet. 2. 21. That implies *all* His steps as He trod this earth as a perfect Man. Was St. Peter thinking again over the three times that our Lord had said to him: "Follow Me"? Some of you are already saying: "Yes, it's all very well repeating Scripture: but tell us how it is to be done!" Well, first ask yourself: "Have I ever really *tried* to do so?" Be quite honest about it. For instance, do you know your Bible well enough to know what those steps are? Or have we even asked the Lord Jesus to reveal them? If not, why not be silent before Him and pray:

> "Lord, let me see Thy footsteps,
>   And in them plant my own:
> My hope to follow duly,
>   Is in Thy strength alone."

Let us say with the Psalmist: "I will run the way of Thy commandments, when Thou shalt enlarge my heart", Psa. 119. 32. When the Lord spake to Moses "face to face, as a man speaketh to his friend, Moses said to Him, Now therefore I pray Thee . . . shew me now Thy way, that I may know Thee . . . And He said, My presence shall go with Thee, and I will give thee rest", Exod. 33. 11-14. *We* have the presence of the Lord Jesus always with us— dwelling in us. *He* will guide *our* steps.

There are an increasing number of people to-day who

are longing for a clearer knowledge of God. A young friend of mine, with a number of others, held an open-air service in a poor London parish. At the close, he invited the crowd into a Mission Hall for a Gospel meeting. As they began to march in, my friend tackled a boy of fifteen, and said: "Will you come to our meeting in the Hall?" "Not I," was the quick answer: *"Religion's no good.* I sang in St. M——'s choir till my voice broke. Was baptised and confirmed, and all that; but a lot of good it did me! No—there's nothing in it. And *now* I'm wondering if there *is* a God at all. Look here, sir, if only God would come down out of His heaven and let us see what He's like, I'd follow him." (He *found out* before the meeting was over.) But God *has* come down, as the Man Christ Jesus. Our Saviour is very God of very God. God *made man.* Jesus Christ is God . . . "manifest in the flesh", 1 Tim. 3. 16. *We know* what God is like.

And not only did the Father "send" Christ Jesus "into the world", but in the same way, and for the same PURPOSE, our Lord has sent *us* into the world. John 17. 21; 20. 21. The same way? Yes, and we *fail* so often by forgetting this. Christ's "steps" were all guided and controlled by God the Father Who dwelt in Christ. He could say, "I and the Father are One", John 10. 30.

Read again John 14. 7-12. Think over that great truth and startling PROMISE, ver. 12. You and I are "sent" in like manner. "Your life is hid with Christ in God", Col. 3. 3. "Self" is to be hidden so that Christ may be *seen.* Our desire is so to hold up the picture of Christ Jesus that not even our finger-tips are seen.

> "Keep me shining, Lord, keep me shining Lord,
>   In all I say and do;
>   That the world may see, Christ dwells in me
>   And learn to love Him too."

Now for your question: "How can I follow His steps?" there are three things necessary in order to follow Him.

(1) We must know what these "steps" are. This implies and requires a knowledge of the Word of God. Bible reading is of the utmost importance. It gives our Lord great joy to *guide* us. We learn *that* from the Scriptures. "The steps of a good man are ordered by the Lord: and *He delighteth in his way*", Psa. 37. 23. God loves us very dearly, and has done all that it is possible for Him to do to show us His way, and to enable— *empower*—us to walk in it. But He expects us to learn from His Holy Word what that "way" is that He has mapped out for us.

We must store our hearts and minds with the Word of God. Even David knew this. Did he not say: "Thy word have I hid in my heart that I might not sin against Thee"? He is writing to *young men*, for he says, "Wherewithal shall a young man cleanse his way? by taking heed thereto according to Thy word", Psa. 119. 9.

Think of Simon Peter's wonderful words which the Holy Spirit inspired him to write:

"Grace and peace be multiplied unto you through the KNOWLEDGE of God and of Jesus our Lord, according as His divine power hath given unto us *all things* that pertain unto life and godliness, through the KNOWLEDGE of Him Who hath called us to GLORY and virtue: Whereby are given unto us exceeding great and precious promises, that by these ye might be *partakers of the Divine nature*", 2 Peter 1. 2-4.

(2) We must truly *love* our Saviour, if we are to desire to "imitate" Him. Now we have already seen that we cannot *make* ourselves love Him. No! And the Bible tells us this also. "We love Him, because He first loved us", 1 John 4. 19. That is why we said so much about "His great love wherewith He loved us", Eph. 2. 4, in earlier chapters. "Thy love to me was wonderful", 2 Sam. 1. 26. And when we truly love HIM He will be our greatest HERO, leading us on to heroic deeds for Him.

(3) Christ Jesus must dominate our THOUGHT-LIFE. Failure on our part to allow Him to possess our thoughts is really the source of all sin. But unless we know His promises, His power, and, above all, His love, we can have but few "thoughts" concerning Him. We have *His* thoughts, concerning us—all of them "thoughts of peace," and a never-failing purpose that all that He allows to happen to us is for our highest good and greatest joy, Jer. 29. 11. When we are deeply in love with anyone it is impossible to go for long *without* thinking of them. When a surprise *"joy"*, or bit of good news, or any amusing incident comes our way, our first thought is, "I must tell ——". Our friends, and even casual acquaintances, soon discover our secret. "Oh, he's simply wrapped up in her", or she in *him*. Do *our* friends ever say about us, "He is simply 'wrapped up' in Christ Jesus"? or "in religion"? Do not reply by saying, "My work is very exacting, and needs mental concentration all the time".

For instance, here is a young man "over head and ears in love". He wants to marry, but cannot afford it. Does this make him "slap-dash" and careless about his work in the office, factory, or shop? Far from it! The reverse is the case. He works all the harder and all the better, so that his foreman or manager, or employer, may be impressed with his value and raise his salary. And as he works away with greater vigour than before, his mind is constantly reverting to his beloved. His better work is done for *her* sake. And when we are "over head and ears" in love for Christ Jesus, that queer expression will have a fresh meaning, our heads will be constantly occupied with thoughts of *Him*, and our ears—spiritual "ears"—ever open to receive messages from Him. Yet, again let it be said, this will be difficult unless we know our Bibles, and "let the word of Christ" dwell in us richly, Col. 3. 16. If a youth finds an incentive to better work when he "falls in love", surely *we* shall do so when we "rise in love"—love to our Saviour, Who so freely gives us all things? *Think* of His promise, "Lo, I am with you alway", Matt. 28. 20.

> "Take my thoughts and let them be
> Dedicated, Lord, to Thee:
> Ever getting from above
> Revelations of Thy love."

The Saviour craves for our love, and longs to dwell in our thoughts. It truly passeth understanding why He should do so, and we ought to rejoice with exceeding great joy to know His great regard for us.

There is a well-known hymn of which every verse ends with the couplet:

> "Jesus, my Lord, I Thee adore;
> O *make* me love Thee more and more."

Is God able to *make* us love Him? For love is never the result of effort or compulsion. But we must not forget that "the love of God is shed abroad in our hearts *by the Holy Ghost* which is given unto us", Rom. 5. 5; and God will, by all the means in His power, endeavour to persuade us; yes, and even *make* us receive and respond to that love, even if He has to send *tribulation* upon us to secure it, ver. 3. God will never rest content with our keeping all His other commandments, if we refuse to obey the first and *great* commandment: "Thou shalt love the Lord Thy God with all thy heart, and with all thy soul, and with all thy MIND, and with all thy strength", Mark 12. 30.

The greatest condemnation our Lord uttered over the very religious, but self-righteous Pharisees, was that they "passed over . . . the LOVE OF GOD", Luke 11. 42.

But we must not spend our time thinking over our poor love to Him and wondering if we love Him enough to *merit* all His promises. Rather may we pray:

> "Lord, it is my chief complaint
> That my love is cold and faint;
> Yet I love Thee, and adore—
> O for grace to love Thee more."

We may learn from Scripture what the Saviour's "steps" are that we are to follow, and we may safely trust His promises. God cannot lie.

"Thou wilt keep him in perfect peace whose mind is stayed on thee; because he trusteth in Thee", Isa. 26. 3. And what was God's answer? "I the Lord do keep it; I will water it every moment; lest any hurt it. I will keep it night and day", Isa. 27. 3. It is when we "Rejoice in the Lord alway" and are "careful"—anxious—"for nothing", because we *know* that God has promised to supply all our need, that "the peace of God which passeth all understanding shall KEEP our hearts and minds through Christ Jesus", Phil. 4. 4, 6, 7, 19.

In these days of stress and strain we need *God's peace* in our hearts and MINDS as never before. The word KEEP means *to garrison* our minds. *He* can control our thought-life if we allow Him to do so.

The more we know about Christ Jesus, the easier will it be to keep Him in our thoughts. Read St. Paul's Epistles—especially the shorter ones. Again and again he prays that his converts and disciples should *know* the Saviour better. "And this I pray, that your LOVE may abound yet more and more in KNOWLEDGE", Phil. 1. 9. God has declared that a glorious day will come when "They shall teach no more every man his neighbour, and every man his brother, saying, KNOW the Lord: for they shall all know Me, from the least of them unto the greatest of them", Jer. 31. 34.

Let us take care to remember that God delights to share our joys as well as our sorrows. Two delightful illustrations of this have come to my notice. A lady in a lovely Surrey country town, bought some new shoes for her small child. The next morning the little maiden gave her mother no rest until the shoes were put on and the little one started

off for a walk. As they passed the church, the child said,
"Mummy, is the church open?" "Oh, yes, darling,"
was the reply. "Then I must go in," exclaimed the little
one. Mother opened the door and followed her child
into the sacred building, wondering what was going to
take place. The child walked up the aisle until she
reached the communion rails. Then she lifted one foot
on to the cushion and looking up to the roof, said, "Lord
Jesus, I want you to see my new shoes. *Thank* you,
Jesus".

During my stay in India I found the children there
very fond of their Bibles. The Lord Jesus was a real
Friend, in their eyes. During a football match between
two Mission Schools, the centre forward of one team shot
a magnificent goal just before the whistle sounded—the
winning goal, for the scores were level before. As the
ball sped toward a certain goal, he cried in a joyous voice:
"*Deko! Yesu Swami. Deko!*" "Look! Jesus the greatest
one, Look"! (*Swami* is the highest title possible).

Let us take our joys to Jesus to share as well as our
sorrows.

> "Jesus is with me, with me to-day;
> With me at work, and with me at play.
> Jesus is with me wherever I go—
> Oh how I love Him Who loveth me so."

CHAPTER XXI

The Most Wonderful Words

HAVE we lost the sense of WONDER? "The trouble is," said Newman, "you do not meditate, and therefore you are not impressed". The most wonderful words ever spoken, and the most wonderful things ever written, are to be found in the 17th chapter of John. And yet, it is quite probable that many of us who have a great love and reverence for our Saviour have never even read it and certainly have never meditated over that amazing prayer.

These remarks are not made in an unkindly or criticising spirit, for I must confess that for many years I have felt no "wonder" or astonishment on reading that chapter, or ever preached a sermon on any verse in it. Yet in those priceless twenty-six verses we hear the Son of God in close intimate personal communion with God the Father. He allows his closest friends to hear as He reveals the thoughts of His heart. That fact alone is sufficient to make that utterance one of profoundest interest and importance. But when we realise that seven times over our Lord speaks of us—*of you* and of me—our wonder should excite our deepest interest. What has the Saviour to tell the Father about *me*? And why should the Lord Jesus *need* to tell Him about *me*? There is not any creature "that is not manifest in His sight, but all things are naked and opened unto the eyes of Him with Whom we have to do", Heb. 4. 13.

Look once again at just half a sentence in a prayer offered up for YOU more than 1900 years ago—a prayer

159

from the heart and lips of the Son of God: "Neither pray I for these alone" (*i.e.* My inner circle of disciples), "but for them also that shall believe on me through their word", John 17. 20.

Well might we be amazed at such forethought on our behalf. But the wonder of it all! A prayer for *me*, so unworthy of it, so needful of it. Shall it, *can* it, be in vain? St. Paul said, "I am crucified with Christ, nevertheless I live; yet not I, but Christ liveth in me. . . . I do NOT FRUSTRATE the grace of God", Gal. 2. 20-21. And God forbid that either you or I should do so. Let us, rather, re-dedicate ourselves to God, "in full and glad surrender". Shall we not do it?

> "In full and glad surrender
>   I give myself to Thee;
> Thine utterly and only,
>   And evermore to be.
> "O Son of God, Who lov'st me,
>   I will be Thine alone,
> And all I have, and all I am
>   Shall henceforth be Thine own.
> "O, come and reign, Lord Jesus:
>   Rule over *everything*;
> And KEEP ME always loyal,
>   And true to Thee, my KING."
>
>   FRANCES R. HAVERGAL

43420